The Destruction of America Is Coming Soon

The Destruction of America Is Coming Soon
Where Is America in the Bible?

iUniverse books may be ordered through booksellers or by contacting:

iUniverse
1663 Liberty Drive
Bloomington, IN 47403
www.iuniverse.com
1-800-Authors (1-800-288-4677)

ISBN: 978-1-4620-1945-8 (sc)
ISBN: 978-1-4620-1948-9 (ebk)

Library of Congress Control Number: 2011909017

Scripture references are from the King James Bible[1].
All Scripture quotations are shown in boldface.
Italicized words are used for emphasizing something being taught.
Words shown in parentheses are a help for the reader to understand scriptural words and other words used in the book.

Cover Design by William Gray

Printed in the United States of America

iUniverse rev. date: 06/25/2011

THE DESTRUCTION OF AMERICA IS COMING SOON

Where Is America in the Bible?

WILLIAM R. GRAY

iUniverse, Inc.
Bloomington

CONTENTS

Preface

I was a pastor of the Maumee Bible Church for fourteen years in Maumee, Ohio, from 1977 through 1990. During that time, I taught a lot about what the Bible says concerning prophecy, which has to do with the Bible's predictions about past things that were predicted and came to pass and things that are predicted concerning the future things in this world that will soon happen. I was taught these things about prophecy from pastors, prophecy teachers, authors of Christian books, and teachers on Christian TV and radio stations. These teachers were wrong about several things they taught, and I was blind to this because I put my trust in their many college degrees and the fact that they were well-known in the Christian community. I failed to check out their teachings and didn't study the Bible enough to see their errors.

About 98 to 99 percent of the Christian church today believes that the Antichrist will come from the European common market nations. This belief has come from same teachers we have believed in and sat under. I believed the same thing, and it caused me to get on a bandwagon in 1988 and believe that the Lord Jesus Christ was coming back in that year to take his church up in what is called the rapture. When he didn't come for his church, I was both disappointed and let down. Fifteen years later, the Lord allowed me to experience a TIA, which is a minor stroke, and I spent the next six months in a recliner chair doing nothing at first but watching TV. After a couple of weeks of wasting my time, I decided to do some Bible study on prophecy and find out why I had been deceived.

I really studied deeply into Bible prophecy and spent more time in the Word of God than I had ever done during the time I was a pastor. I spent hour after hour digging into the books of Revelation, Daniel, Jeremiah, Ezekiel, Zechariah, and Isaiah. I both learned and found new and different interpretations from the Scriptures than had been taught to me in the past. I found out in the study of the seventeenth chapter of the book of Revelation that the Antichrist comes from the seventh head of the beast, and he brings in the ten kings and is the eighth head who rules in the coming world government system. Also, I learned in Isaiah 14 that he rules from end-time Babylon, not the European Union. That is totally different than we have been taught by today's Bible prophecy teachers. So with that, let's do an in-depth Bible study together.

This book is a result my study of the Scriptures concerning end-time prophecy. It comes entirely from the Bible, without any help from any other book about prophecy, but it will include a few quotes that will enrich what the Word of God teaches. What is contained in here will startle many people, and they'll want to deny it because of their preconceived ideas concerning the end times and their belief that the United States is not mentioned in the Scriptures. The Bible is so very clear that the United States is end-time Babylon in the Scriptures, and this book will reveal that fact and accurate details about the soon-coming destruction of our beloved country.

My prayer is that anyone reading this will pick up the Word of God and follow me through the Scriptures. I do not believe the Bible teaches that the world will end, but instead it teaches us about the end of the human government systems and our Lord's return to the earth to set up his government over man, with him ruling. Remember the words of our Lord's Prayer that many of you reading have repeated throughout your lifetime. Part of it says, **"Thy kingdom come, thy will be done, on Earth as it is in heaven."** This is a reference to the millennial kingdom of a thousand years. This kingdom is just around the corner and will most likely begin before the end of the year 2020.

I know it is going to be hard for most of you to believe this, but our beloved country that had its roots in Christianity *will **not*** be in existence when our Lord returns to set up his kingdom. This nation of ours is no longer a nation that believes in the Bible, and it has turned its back on our Lord Jesus Christ. It still remains the best nation to live in and still allows us to have our freedoms at this present time, but that will soon end when a one-world government is ushered in, most likely this year, or next. We will slowly but surely lose our precious freedoms that we have now.

Those who believe and trust in today's leadership will be deceived and follow the path of destruction. Many of them will accept the Antichrist as the savior of the world and follow his instructions to take a mark (digital implant) in their right hand or forehead in order to buy or sell anything. This mark, as the Bible calls it, will look like it's the answer for all of the problems of planet Earth but instead will cause its doom. The new world government will bring in a world currency first, and then shortly after it comes into existence, they will offer a cashless society, a way to protect your money by voluntarily taking a digital implant in your hand or forehead. It will operate like the current debit card, and then within one and a half years, it will be enforced upon all the people of our nation and the world. At that time, it will be known by the people who have turned to Jesus Christ for salvation as the mark of the beast.

This book is being written as a warning to all Americans who cherish their lives. I love you all and pray that you will see the truth before it's too late. Turn to the God of the Bible who is willing to save you from the destruction that is soon coming upon you. Jesus Christ died for your sins and wants you to repent, which is a 180-degree turn around from you to him. He has promised to change your life by living on the inside of you. Stop following the path that leads to destruction and invite him in! Read Proverbs 3:4–5, **"Trust in the Lord with *all* thine heart, and lean not unto thine own understanding. In *all* thine ways acknowledge him, and he shall direct thy paths."**

Chapter 1

How to Study the Bible through
the Exegetical Process

This book will reveal some of the false doctrines that have been taught to us by pastors, authors, and television prophecy programs and their teachers. It wasn't written to attack the teachers but to reveal the truth from the use of the Scriptures that some of their teachings are in error. We'll do this through the study of the Scriptures using the exegetical process. Pay close attention to the following teaching, because this is the way our Lord has intended us to study his Word. Our Lord has written his Word in such a way that we, when studying it, can find other related Scriptures as proof of the interpretation that he is revealing to us in a given text. We must remember to take out what is revealed in the text and not read into it, for when we take out what is in the text or verse, we are doing what is called an *exegesis* of the Scriptures. That is the only way that our Lord intended us to study His word.

The opposite way to study a given text is to read into it what we believe it might be saying. This is called an *eisegesis*, and it is the method that Satan and his host of fallen angels use to teach us false doctrines. It causes us to study the Scriptures and interpret them by reading into the Scriptures what we think they are saying without comparing the text with other Scriptures that would agree or disagree with our interpretation. The following is the definition of the word exegesis: "**Exegesis:** 1610s, from Gk. exegeisthai 'explain, interpret,' from ex—'out' + hegeisthai 'to lead, guide, seek" [2](from the *Gale Dictionary*). The word exegesis means to draw the meaning *out* of a given text, and exegesis may be contrasted with eisegesis, which means to read one's own interpretation into a given text. In general, exegesis presumes an attempt to view the text objectively, while eisegesis implies one is viewing it more subjectively.

When studying, we first need to examine the general historical and cultural context, along with confirming the limits of the passage, and then examine the context within the text. We must also take into consideration the verses before and after the one we are looking at. It involves a process of a private study or task in which the Bible student examines the backgrounds, meanings, and forms of the words, looks at who is speaking in a given text, who are he or she is talking to, and what is being said before and after a verse of Scripture. The exegete seeks to comprehend the exact meaning of a Bible passage studied. When studying this way, we must remember that it is not through our intellect that we will comprehend what a passage of a given text is teaching but what the Lord reveals to us through our effort of laboring in his Word to discover his truth. We must study the Scriptures with an open mind to receive the truth. By open mind, I do not mean that we are to read a text and just sit there waiting for the Lord to fill it. I mean we are to drop all of our preconceived ideas about what we have been taught so that the Lord is able to give us understanding concerning what he is saying.

We live in the day and time when the apostle Paul told Timothy in 2 Timothy 4:2–4—"**Preach the word; be instant** (ready) **in season, out of season; reprove rebuke, exhort with all long suffering and doctrine. For the time will come when they will not endure sound doctrine, but after their own lusts** (desires) **shall they heap to themselves teachers, having itching ears. And they shall turn away their ears from the truth, and shall be turned unto fables**"—to teach the truth, because the *day would come* that people (Christians) would *not* endure sound doctrine, but they would seek teaching they desired. Paul went on to say in verse four that they would turn from the truth and desire to hear fables, meaning stories. We must approach our Lord with humility while seeking for knowledge and understanding concerning his Word. We need to remember that his Holy Spirit indwells us (believers), and through our labor in God's Word, he will teach us. John 14:26 says, **"But the Comforter, who is the Holy Spirit, whom the Father will send in my name, he shall teach you all things . . ."**

Scripture tells us that that we don't have any wisdom in and of ourselves to understand what the Scriptures are teaching. First Corinthians 3 tells us we are to become fools that we might become wise. First Corinthians 3:18–21 says, **"Let no man deceive himself. If any man among you seemeth to be wise in this world, let him become a fool, that he may be wise. For the *wisdom* of this world is *foolishness* with God. For it is written, He taketh the wise in their own craftiness. And again, The Lord knoweth the thoughts of the wise, that they are vain. Therefore let no man glory in men. For all things are yours."**

People often use their own wisdom for an interpretation of a given text. Many born-again Christians are guilty of this, including myself when I failed to study the Scriptures back in 1988. I read into them what I had first read in the commentaries concerning prophecy, and I was not trusting in the Lord but putting into Scripture the things authors had written. I believed them because their many years of study, along with the fact that they had several degrees and they were well-known authors. We as Christians today need to have the spiritual attitude of the early church at Berea, for the Scriptures say of them in Acts 17:11, **"These were more noble than those in Thessalonica, in that they received the word with all readiness of mind, and searched the Scriptures daily, whether those things were so."**

One Christian believer told me that when his Sunday service is over, about half or more of the members leave their Bibles in the pews until the next service and that this is done continually. By the way, this is a fundamental Bible-believing and -teaching church. Not only are Christians not getting deeper into Bible study, but most of them don't study the Bible at all, and when they do accept an interpretation of Scripture, it's usually one that they have been taught. They accept it without checking out the Scriptures to see if it is true. You might say that they are just floating along with their teachers. Those who fail to spend a lot of time in the Scriptures are guilty of the above.

We don't need degrees or human wisdom to rightly divide the truth in the Bible. I'm not saying that we don't need good teachers, but that their degrees obtained through seminaries and Bible colleges do not guarantee that we will receive the correct interpretation of the Scripture. When taking a stand, such as I have, in exposing their false teachings that I have corrected with the Scriptures, I'm sure they believe I'm a very critical person who doesn't drift along with the end-time prophecy doctrines that the vast majority of the church believes are correct. Due to their lack of study in the Scriptures containing prophecy, most pastors would view *me* as a person teaching false doctrine.

In April 2009, I visited a church in Columbia, South Carolina, and sat under a pastor who had the title of doctor before his name. In the first twenty-five minutes, he took one verse of Scripture in 1 Corinthians 13 completely out of context and taught that it was referring to today's Christians who see in a mirror darkly. Then he went on to teach us that it was the way we see today concerning the relationships in a married couple's life. He then began to give us some guidelines to follow that would help us in our relationship with our spouses. There were two services that day of about fifteen hundred to two thousand people each, or around four thousand people total, who didn't heard the Word of God taught correctly. In fact, all they heard that morning was false doctrine being taught because a verse of Scripture taken out of context is a pretext, and a pretext is a lie.

The verse he used was verse 12, **"For now we see through a glass [mirror] darkly; but then face to face: now I know in part; but then shall I know even as also I am known."** If a person keeps this verse in context, he/she will see that that statement only applied to the Christians of Paul's day, and it has nothing to do with us today. We today can see very clearly, as we have all of the books of the New Testament, but they saw things darkly, because they did not have anywhere near all of them at the time when the apostle Paul wrote the letter to them in AD 55. It wasn't until AD 95-100 that they had the completed New Testament, and that is why they saw in a mirror darkly. In this text, Paul is telling them why they still have some of the temporary gifts that God was using in his infant church, which would be taken away when the *perfect* (complete) seen in verse 10 came. The Greek word for perfect in verse 10 means complete or mature. In fact, chapters 12 and 13 are both talking about the spiritual gifts given in the body of Christ in that day and time. The word perfect used in this text means the completed Word of God.

You must study the Scriptures along with me through this book to see where the Bible predicts the total destruction of our beloved America. You must be willing to look at the Scriptures using the exegesis format, or you will not see the truth. First, there are many verses we must examine in the Scriptures before revealing the fact that America is end-time Babylon. Understanding of these verses is also needed to see who the major end-time players are.

Chapter 2

Why We Haven't Heard the United States Mentioned in the Bible

We have been taught several false things about prophecy concerning who the major end time players are. Here are some of them:

- There isn't any mention of America in the Bible.

- The United States will dwindle in power, and thus she will not be a key player in end-time prophecy.

- America will be defeated by war and will no longer be a power.

- America will suffer an economic collapse and will dwindle in power.

- The Antichrist will rule the world from and along with ten nations from the current European Common Market, and it, the ECM, will be the leader of the end-times' One-World Government . . .

- The woman sitting on the beast in Revelation is the Roman Catholic Church or America.

Satan has used these false teachings to keep the world blind to the role America plays in prophecy concerning the end time. Remember, he is the great deceiver who the Bible says deceives the whole world.

The definition of the Beast in Bible prophecy is the New World Order or the Antichrist, who is the leader of it. It was in existence once *before* during the time when the Tower of Babel ruled over all the people of planet Earth and they were united together against God and worshipping all of the false gods instead of the true God of the Bible. The Lord commanded them to fill and replenish the earth, but they stayed in one area. God came down and separated them by giving them different languages and scattered them over the face of the earth to make it more difficult for Satan to get them together again as one.

Satan went to work on getting them united again for the sole purpose of getting them away from God and eventually worship him. He started with Egypt and then Assyria as world empires and then with the following nations that ruled the world: Babylon, Medo-Persia, Greece, and Rome, with each gathering more land mass than the preceding empire. To become an empire, every one of these nations had to defeat the current empire by force through war, such as when Rome defeated the Grecian empire. We are on the brink of seeing Satan's plan come to fruition, with all the nations of the world united together again in a *one*-world government. This government will come with the reappearance the beast of the days of the Tower of Babel when all the people were united together with Satan in power. We are very likely to see it come into existence in the next couple of years or by the year of 2012.

To reveal what the Bible says about America we need to look into the word of God in Revelation chapter 17 and 1. identify the woman riding the beast; 2. discover who the beast is; 3. identify the mountains; 4. identify the heads on the beast; 5. on which head the ten horns are; 6. when the beast—**"was, is not, and shall be . . ."**— was in existence, and will be in the near future, in existence again. In Revelation 17:5, we see a woman riding on the beast with a message written on her forehead that says: **"MYSTERY BABYLON THE GREAT, THE MOTHER OF HARLOTS AND ABOMINATIONS OF THE EARTH."** In verse 7, an angel tells John, **"I will tell thee the mystery of the woman and of the beast that carrieth her, which hath seven heads and ten horns."** Verse 8 says, **"The beast that thou sawest was, and is not, and shall ascend out of the bottomless pit . . ."** There are *two* Mystery Babylons, one spiritual and one commercial. We'll deal with the spiritual Babylon in this chapter of Revelation. This revealing will take some time in studying the scriptures.

Back to the Revelation chapter 17, this was spoken to John on the island of Patmos by Jesus Christ around AD 90-95, so the tenses must be determined from the time of John's writing the things that he saw. The present tense would be the time he was on the island of Patmos and the angel said that the beast was not during John's time on Patmos, and what empire was in existence at that time? Answer: Rome! Wow, this is so very important if you want to rightly divide the Scriptures and find out who the beast is. Almost every prophecy teacher teaches there will be a revival of the old Roman Empire and that will be the place where the Antichrist rules from. But the beast or the one-world government that will rule in the last days was in existence before the Roman Empire ruled the world and shall be in existence after the collapse of the Roman Empire.

The false teaching that says the revived Roman Empire will rule the world during the tribulation period is taken from verses nine and ten, where it says, **"And here is the mind which hath wisdom. The seven heads are seven mountains** (kingdoms) **on which the woman sitteth."** The teaching is that these seven mountains are the seven hills that Rome is seated on. Let me ask you a question: how did mountains become hills, and how much wisdom did that take? Take a closer look at this text in Revelation 17, and we will discover it to be totally *symbolic* (figurative). So what are these mountains if they are not the hills on which Rome is seated on? When we see a symbolic text, we must dig into the Scriptures to find the answer and remember to look at that text figuratively and not literally. Now let's find out what these mountains figuratively represent.

We will find the answer in the writings of the prophets. Isaiah 13:1–2 says, **"Lift up your banner upon the high *mountain* . . ."** This is a continuation of what was said concerning Babylon in verse 1, and notice the nation or kingdom is referred to as a mountain. Daniel 2:35 also says, **"And the stone that smote the image became a great *mountain* and filled the whole earth."** This stone is not Christ, as we have been taught, and we will see this in detail later in the study of a false doctrine that has been taught to us for years. This stone is the current nation of Israel, and it will become a mountain when Christ sets up His Kingdom in Jerusalem, and it will fill the whole earth.

Remember the Lord's Prayer in the book of Matthew. Matthew 6:10 says, **"Thy Kingdom come. Thy will be done, in earth as it is in heaven."** That is the kingdom being spoken of in the book of Revelation. This chapter is covering the nation of Israel in 12:1–6, and in Revelation 12:5, **"And she brought forth a man child** [Jesus]**, who was to rule all nations with a rod of iron: and her** [Israel's] **child was caught up** [a reference to the ascension] **unto God, and to his throne."** Psalm 67:4 says, **"O let the nations be glad and sing for joy: for thou shalt judge the people righteously, and govern the nations upon earth."** Christ will rule as the king of all the earth from the nation of Israel.

Some more examples of nations being called mountains are seen in Jeremiah 51:24–25 when it speaks about Babylon: **"I will render unto Babylon . . . Behold, I am against thee, O destroying *mountain* . . . and will make thee a burnt *mountain*."** This is referring to the destruction of *end-time* Babylon, which will be burned when it is destroyed, according to Revelation 18:18, **"And cried when they saw the smoke of her burning . . ."** and Jeremiah 50:32, **"I will kindle a fire in his cities, and it shall devour all round about him."** David in Psalm 30, while describing how the Lord has turned his mourning into dancing in verse 11, says, **"Lord, by thy favor thou hast made my *mountain* [kingdom] to stand strong . . ."** He wasn't referring to a mass of dirt and rocks, but to his kingdom that the Lord had made him a king over, the nation of Israel.

Other verses that show mountains symbolically as nations or kingdoms are Isaiah 2:2, 11:9, and 25:10. Thus nations or kingdoms are called *mountains*, except where the Scripture demands a literal interpretation. Now, let's go back to the text in Revelation 17, and we will see how the Scripture looks when it's rightly divided. In verses 9 through 11, we see the woman sitting on the beast that has seven mountains representing seven kingdoms, and since she is the mother of all harlots, she has to be from the place that started all the false religions, or gods, or the birthplace of all the anti-God teachings. That can only be one place: the Tower of Babel, which can rightly be labeled "the first Babylon," or the *first Beast*. She is religious Babylon, as we see from her title in Revelation 17:5, **"MYSTERY BABYLON THE GREAT, THE MOTHER OF HARLOTS** [false religions] **AND ABOMINATIONS OF THE EARTH."**

The key word in this verse is *mother*, and we see that she gave birth to all the harlots (false gods or religions). When thinking about a city, keep this in your mind: it's not the buildings that make up the city but the civil and religious authorities that constitute, or make up, what is called a city. In this text, the woman representing Babylon is the religious authority of a city in the past, *not Rome*. Rome was not the mother who gave birth to all the false gods and goddesses, but she did have the woman called Mystery Babylon sitting on her, just as all the past world kingdoms did, and so will mountain number seven when it comes into power. It will be a kingdom that will unite all the false gods into a one-world religion and give freedom to the people to worship any god they want to, other than Jesus Christ.

We will look at the other authority, the civil side of Babylon, when we come to commercial Babylon in Revelation 18, but for now take notice that the woman is sitting on the nations, past, present, and future, and that these nations were world empires. This is seen in 17:10 with the words, **"And there are seven kings . . ."** Do not take these out of context, and try make them seven past kings of the Roman empire, for these are the past, present, and future world empires that she is seated on, and the present one of John's time, while he was in exile on Patmos, was the Roman Empire. The word for kings in the Greek language means, "A foundation of power, sovereign, or king," and it can be translated *kingdom*. Now look carefully at the rest of the verse, **"Five are fallen, one is, and the other is not yet come."** Thus, keeping in mind the Tower of Babel, or the first Babylon, as it was the *beast that was*, and going forward in history, here is a list of the world empires from that point forward:

1. Egypt
2. Assyria
3. Babylon, the second one
4. Mede Persia
5. Greece. That makes five that have fallen, *past*. I've italicized the tenses.
6. Rome, which was in power in John's day while in exile on the island of Patmos, would be the *present* of the day and time he was writing.
7. America, which will bring in the 8th head with ten horns (one-world government)

The first five kingdoms already ruled in the *past* (John's time on Patmos) and Rome was in existence at that time (*present*). One kingdom is yet to come and it is the *future* seventh head, and when it does it brings in the eight head.

End-time Babylon is Mystery Babylon, the seventh head or kingdom, and it will be revealed later in the study. You will find it to be the *future* kingdom that will bring in the last world government system. I don't have time in this Bible study to go back and cover all the false religions that came out of Babel, but the primary one was the worship of the mother as supreme god with her son as a young child. While the names of the gods and goddesses changed after the Lord scattered them over the face of the earth at the Tower of Babel, the essential elements of pagan idolatry were exactly alike. Babel was not one of the world empires but the birthplace of the beast *that was* in Revelation 17, and it was the *first* world government system. God himself destroyed it, and it was the place where all of the world's pagan religion started. The god that they worshiped was the goddess Ishtar, which was started by Nimrod, and his mother Semaramis, whom he later married. Nimrod, being a hunter of men, began to bring them together in *one area*, and by doing so, they were rebelling against the Lord who had commanded them to replenish (fill all the earth) with people. Nimrod's name means *rebel.*

Satan used three things to deceive the people and turn them away from the truth.

1. He twisted the promise of God in Genesis 3 about the coming redeemer and put the emphasis on the *woman* while keeping the son an *infant.*

2. He changed and hid the message of God in the stellar heavens (signs in the stars) concerning the gospel by bringing in astrology.

3. He gave the people before the flood a host of fallen angels who took upon themselves the bodies of men so that they could marry the women and destroy the whole human race through an ungodly mixture of angels and humanity, and the offspring that were born from this mix were giants. They were noble in their day, and the people worshiped the angelic beings as gods that came down from heaven.

We can even see that during the day when the apostle Paul was in Lystra and healed a lame man. In Acts 14:8–12, Paul **"Said With a loud voice, Stand upright on thy feet, And he leaped and walked. And when the people saw what Paul had done, they lifted up their voices, saying in the speech of Lycaonia, The gods are come down to us in the likeness of men."** It was just like those at Babel and before the flood thought that the fallen angels were gods that came down from above, and they worshiped them. And by the way, Nimrod, who hunted men to worship these false gods, was the great grandson of Noah. Ham, Noah's son, was the father of Cush, who was the father of Nimrod.

Notice that it didn't take long before the false gods on the other side of the flood were being worshipped again. There were eight people on the ark, but only one in the Scriptures is mentioned as being righteous with God, and that was Noah. His offspring knew about the false gods, and began to teach them to their children, and they in return taught them to their children, and so on. Satan had them worshiping the gods of the heavens instead of the Lord who made the heavens. Now let's look at the nations and the false deities they worshipped following the scattering of the people by our Lord at Babel:

1. Egypt had many gods and goddesses, but the principal goddess was Isis and her son Horus. Isis was known as *Lady* of Heaven, Mighty *Goddess*, and the *Mistress* of the World. Again, just like Babel, Satan has the woman as the great god or goddess (harlot) of a false religion.
2. Assyria had the same goddess as the tower of Babel. Ishtar was her Assyrian name, and later the Hebrews called her Ashtoreth. She is known as the *goddess* who rejoices mankind, the great *goddess*, the *queen* of all gods, and the *mistress* of heaven and earth.
3. Babylon—in this kingdom, she was called Nana, but she is the same goddess as Ishtar and Ashtoreth to the Hebrews.
4. In Medo-Persia, she is called Ishtar again, and like Babylon before them, she is called Nana or Beltis
5. In Greece, she is called Aphrodite, and Eros, also known as Rome's Venus and Cupid. She was also called Artemis. In fact Artemis, Aphrodite of Greece, Anaea and Anaitis of the Persians, and Nana of Babylon are one and the same goddess.
6. Rome had at the time of John's day Jupiter, Mars, and Venus, well known with her child Cupid, Janus, Quirinus, and Juno.
7. In America *the church* is called Roman Catholicism, and they lift up the mother *Mary* and Jesus her child as their primary way of worship. This form of religion is wrong, because it comes from the false gods of the past with the worship of the *mother* being more important than Jesus.

Note, because the mother with child has been worshipped down through the centuries, that is also why Christmas is a very popular holiday with non-Christians as well as believers. As long as Satan can keep Jesus Christ as a baby, he knows people will receive him in that capacity, but put him dying on the cross as an adult for their sins, and they immediately reject him.

Now we can see that the woman in Revelation 17 did indeed sit on all of these nations. She was and is religious Babylon who inserts her authority over the kingdoms of this world. She is also sitting on the seventh head, which is the nation (America, the USA) that will usher in the beast of the near future, which is the world government system of the Antichrist that will come upon this earth, which is the eighth head of Revelation 17:11. To find the answer to the false of the teaching of the *Antichrist ruling with ten revived of Roman Empire nations,* we must return to Revelation 17 and remember to not take any verse, or words out of the text.

Let's consider Revelation 17:10–16. Verse 11 says, **"And the beast that *was*, and *is not*, even he is *the eighth*, and is of the seven, and goeth into perdition."** There are two important things to understand in this verse. First: the beast *was* (past tense) before John's time, and *is not* during John's time on the island of Patmos, and *shall be*, is the *eighth* head to come from the *seven*. That is the Beast is a product of the seven kingdoms before it, and the seventh head brings it into existence. Here is the proof from the Word of God that the beast is not the Roman Empire, for Rome was in power during John's exile on Patmos and never had been in existence before, as a world empire. The Scripture clearly says the beast *is not* during John's time. That rules out the Roman Empire as the beast. Also notice that the ten horns in verse 12, **"And the ten horns which thou sawest are ten kings, which have received no kingdom as yet; but receive power as kings one hour with the beast."** They *are* on *the eighth head*, or the head of the beast, which is the revived beast of Babel or end-time Babylon during the tribulation period.

Also notice that these horns have *no kingdom* as yet in verse 12, so they can't be kings of nations in existence such as European nations who have kings already. Please, take a close look at the one hour mentioned in verse 12. It does not say *in one hour,* so do not take the *"one hour"* in verse 12 as a literal sixty minutes. Remember that this text is symbolic, and one hour most likely refers to a very short period of time, as we know that the ten horns or kings will rule with the Antichrist during the tribulation period. Thus the hour most likely means a few years, and you might want to compare this with the half hour of silence in heaven mentioned in Revelation 8:1, where it could possibility mean three and a half years.

This author believes that the ten horns will be ten territorial kings to be selected to rule in the coming one-world government of the beast. The difference between the past world empires and end-time Babylon's kingdom is that the empires of the past world rulers were created or taken by force as they conquered the other nations through war. This last world government system will be assembled by the Antichrist during the peaceful period of the first three and a half years of Daniel's 70th week which is the last seven years of God dealing with the Jews. Why do I believe this? Answer: because Satan wants the world working together as it was in the days of the Tower of Babel, with the original beast, and when people worshipped any god they wanted to. And since those gods are offspring of his demons, their job as Satan's followers is to draw people away from the true God, and that will make it much easier for Satan to turn them toward him during the middle of the tribulation period when he claims to be god. Question: who is the seventh head? Answer: the seventh head on the beast is the last world empire (giant), and it is the nation that will be recognized as end-time Babylon, which the Bible clearly identifies by its *characteristics* is the United States. You will see no mention of the words America or the United States in the Bible, but you will view all of the characteristics of it.

America will play the major part of bringing in a universal, worldwide government system, consisting of the Antichrist as its leader, with ten kings from around the world, and these kings will represent the eighth head on the beast with its ten horns. We will also find out in the Scriptures that the Antichrist will rule the world over these ten kings and that he is from the United States. By the way, we as a nation of people were at first established by people who came here from nations of the old

Roman Empire. So America is a product of the seed from the old Roman Empire. The eagle was used as a symbol of the Roman Empire, and it is the symbol of America. The Senate that America has was inherited from the Roman Empire.

Also, the false prophet who is the end-time religious leader will head up a one-world church during the first three and a half years, which will be covered in the teaching about the little horn in Daniel 7 and Revelation 17. Before going on to the next study of another error, let's recap the five things we learned about Revelation 17.

1. *The identity of the woman:* She is religious Babylon from the tower of Babel who is seated upon seven mountains (nations) that down through the ages have had, and will still in the future have, a great religious influence over the world. She was and is the mother of all harlots, known as false gods and goddesses.

2. *Who the beast is:* It is the first world government of Babel and will also be the final world government system of the tribulation period. That is the beast that was and is not and shall be of Revelation 17.

3. *Identity of the mountains:* They represent the nations that were the world empires in existence from Egypt up to the Roman Empire, with the seventh coming shortly and the eighth (the beast with his ten horns) ruling the world as a one-world government system. Religious Babylon is seated on the first seven but not the eighth, which is when the Antichrist will rule during the last three and a half years of the tribulation period. Notice how Satan used the whore (false church) throughout the ages to keep people from knowing the truth, and then in the middle of the tribulation period, he will destroy her in order to get all, or most, of the deceived to worship him.

4. *Identity of the seven heads:* They represent the kingdoms or the nations above that were world empires. The heads were the kingdoms and their kings who sat in authority during the time that each empire was in existence.

5. *On which head the ten horns are:* They are on the eighth head, which is the revival of a one-world government, similar to the Tower of Babel, which is the Antichrist with his ten kings ruling the world. They are not on the seventh head, which

represents the seventh world empire that will usher in a world government system through the Antichrist and his ten kings. Notice that the seventh head (world empire) never rules the world by itself but is responsible for assembling and putting into place the revival of the world government system called the *"beast"* and also known as the *"eighth head."*

6. *When the beast was in existence and when it will be in existence again:* It was first in existence at the Tower of Babel as a world united under Satan and totally against God, as it included all the people of the world who existed at that time, and it will be in existence again during the tribulation period under Satan, uniting all of the world against the one true God and eventually trying to force everyone to worship the Antichrist as god.

Chapter 3

False Teachings Concerning Prophecy that Have Led Us Astray

First False Teaching: *The city of Babylon mentioned in the book of Revelation is today's Babylon located in Iraq.*

We could spend hours on the things in Scripture that prove the city of Babylon in Iraq is *not* the Babylon mentioned as end-time Babylon. Below, I'll list some of the characteristics of end-time Babylon that easily show us that the two are not the same nation.

1. It is a city or nation that has sea ports, as shown in Revelation 18:17–19, **"And every shipmaster, and all the company in ships, and sailors, and as many as trade by the sea, stood afar off, and cried when they saw the smoke of her burning . . ."**
2. It is a nation that is very rich and makes the merchants that trade with her very rich, for the merchants cry when they see her burning and realize that there will be no one to buy their merchandise anymore. Revelation 18:11 says, **"And the merchants of the earth shall weep and**

mourn over her: for no man buyeth their merchandise anymore . . ."

3. This end-time nation glorifies herself and lives well above the wealth of other nations. Revelation 18:7 says, **"How much she hath glorified herself, and lived deliciously** [luxuriously] **. . ."**

Now, let's put our thinking caps on about the three things mentioned above and try to apply them to the Babylon of Iraq. First, the nearest water to the city of Babylon in Iraq is the Persian Gulf, which is over three hundred miles away. Thus it has no sea ports. Second, it is nowhere near the richest nation or city in the world today that is buying loads of merchandise from merchants via the sea. Third, it is an occupied land by the United States today and is not and cannot glorify itself, nor does she live luxuriously.

End-time Babylon is a nation that will have a lot of God's people in it just before it is destroyed. Revelation 18:4 says, **"Come out of her my people** [Jews, and Gentile tribulation converts] **that ye be not partakers of her sins . . ."** Ask yourself this question: how many Jewish people are presently living in the Babylon of Iraq today, or how many people including Christians believers are living there? Need I say more? The city, other than our present military forces, contains Arabs who are not believers in the Bible. The religion of Iraq is Islam.

4. She has a mother nation in existence at the time of her destruction, so we know that she was birthed from another nation, because of what the Scripture says in Jeremiah 50:12, **"Your mother shall be sore** [deeply] **confounded that bare you shall be ashamed . . ."** So there is in existence today the nation that gave physical birth to end-time Babylon, and Iraq's Babylon was not given birth by another nation.

5. Jeremiah 50:12b says, **"Behold the hindermost of the nations . . ."** Now we see another characteristic of end-time Babylon, as she is said to be the latest or last nation to come into existence or the newest nation. Thus

it cannot be ancient Babylon, for she has been in existence for over twenty-five hundred years.

6. She is the hammer of the whole earth. That is, she builds and reshapes the nations of this planet. She designs them to be what she wants them to be. She is also the leader and builder of the coming one-world government system.

7. She is a very proud nation. Jeremiah 50:31 says, **"O thou most proud . . ."** and she makes a statement that she will never see great harm within her borders, because of her military power. Jeremiah 50:51 says, **"Though Babylon should mount up to heaven, and though she should fortify the height of her strength."** The mentioning of her fortifying her strength up to heaven most likely refers to her military spy network through satellites. Babylon in Iraq is neither a proud city nor has it put satellites in space.

8. She is a nation of mixed or mingled people, or she has a great mixture of people from all the nations. Jeremiah 50:37 says, **"All the mingled people that are in the midst of her . . ."** Does this sound like Iraq's Babylon?

9. She is a nation that is crazy about her idols or loves the wonderful things she has, and those things keep her people from needing God. Jeremiah 50:38 says, **"They are mad** (insane) **upon their idols."**

10. End-time Babylon has a plurality of cities, not just one city as the Babylon of Iraq is today. Jeremiah 50:32 says, **"And I shall kindle a fire in his cities . . ."** There are many other characteristics about end-time Babylon that prove that she and Iraq's Babylon are two separate civil authorities. This will be covered in a separate Bible study in chapter 5, and it will help us identify who Ecclesiastical and Commercial Babylon are.

Second False Teaching: *The toes seen on the image in Daniel 2 represent the revived Roman Empire.*

Looking in Daniel 2:32-43, we see four beasts mentioned, and on the fourth beast we see the toes on the feet of each leg. Daniel 2:42 says, **"And as the toes of the feet were part of iron, and part of clay, so the kingdom shall be partly strong and partly broken."** These toes are not a kingdom in and of themselves, but the bottom part, or the end of the fourth beast, which was the Roman Empire. It was like iron at its beginning, and as it progressed on in time, it separated into two divisions, the eastern and the western legs, and as time went on, they had several different leaders in both divisions. The two divisions of the kingdom are represented by the two legs of the image when it began and at its ending. At the beginning of the empire, the legs were iron, strong and powerful, and at the Roman Empire's ending, we see the bottom of the image with the feet and toes being like iron mixed with miry clay, which had no cohesiveness.

Daniel 2:44 starts out with the words, **"And in the days of these kings shall the God of heaven set up a kingdom..."** Here is where the misinterpretation begins. The last thing described in verses 42 and 43 were the toes of the image, and because of this, the modern-day writers of prophecy read into these verses a revival of the old Roman Empire represented by these ten toes of the image. First, let's remember the rules of studying the Scriptures by the exegetical process and the all-important rule of not reading into the text something that is not there. Now, where do you see the word *ten* in this text? You will not find it, because the whole text is talking about *four* beasts, not ten toes and a revived empire of ten nations.

Arguments for those who teach this interpretation are, **"But we know that the end-time world government system has ten kings ruling with the Antichrist."** Yes, they are right about that teaching, but you can't assume that the ten horns in Revelation 17:11-12, which are on the *head* of the beast, are the toes of this image. But someone might say, "Come on now, everyone knows that at the bottom of an image of a man there would be ten toes." Not so says the Scripture. See 2 Samuel 21:20, which says, **"And there was yet a battle in Gath, where was a man of great stature, that had on every hand six fingers, and on every foot six toes . . ."**

So you see, *assuming* something that is not in the scripture has been the culprit that has led us down the road of misunderstanding the major players of end-time prophecy. Verse 43 of Daniel 2 tells us who the toes were, **"And whereas thou sawest iron mixed with miry clay, they shall *mingle themselves* with the *seed of men*, but they shall not cleave one to another, even as iron is not mixed with clay."** This is the picture of how the fourth beast came to its end. The first leg that came to its end was the western leg in AD 476, and the eastern leg declined until it came to its end in AD 1453. Below is a segment of the Roman Empire's history from AD 305 to 310, and you can get a good look at what was going on with the constant change and the co-ruling of their leaders. There were no single individuals ruling at this time, nor were there any during the latter part of the empire. The following came from the Internet:

> Flavius Julius Constantius, born 31 March AD ca. 250 in Illyricum. Became emperor in 1 May AD 305. Wife: (1) Helena (one son; Constantine), (2) Theodora (two sons; Flavius Dalmatius, Flavius Julius Constantius; third child unknown). Died at Ebucarum (York), 25 July AD 306.Gaius Galerius Valerius Maximianus born AD ca. 250 at Florentiniana, Upper Moesia. Became emperor in 1 May AD 305. Wife: (1) Galeria Valeria (one daughter; Valeria Maximilla), (2) an unknown concubine (one sons; Candidianus). Died at Nicomedia, May AD 311.Flavius Valerius Severus born in the Danubian region, date unknown. Became emperor in August AD 306. Wife: (1) unknown (one son; Severus). Died at Rome, 16 September AD 307.born in AD ca. 279 possibly in Syria. Became emperor in 28 October AD 306. Wife: Valeria Maximilla (two sons; Valerius

Romulus; unknown). Died at Milvian Bridge at Rome, 28 October AD 312.Gaius Galerius Valerius Maximinus born 20 November AD 270 in the Danubian region. Became emperor in 1 August AD 310. Wife: unknown (one daughter; unknown). Died at Tarsus July/August AD 313.[4]

Notice the different areas that each emperor was ruling in, and remember that this represents just the western leg, as the split came in AD 286, as mentioned below. Here we see rulers of different territories, such as: Illyricum, Florentiniana, Danubian, and Syria. Just as the Word of God says, at the bottom of the image, which represents the end of the Roman Empire, there was a mixing in of the rulers across the land mass with the people, and that system didn't work, because iron (the leaders) mixed with clay (the common people) and eventually failed, and the Roman Empire came to its end.

Below is a picture of what was happening just before the above years of AD 305-310, quoted also from the Internet article:

Diocletian was an organizer. In AD 286 he split the empire into east and west, and appointed a Dalmatian colleague, Maximian (d. AD 305), to rule the west and Africa. A further division of responsibilities followed in AD 292. Diocletian and Maximian remained senior emperors, with the title of Augustus, but Galerius, Diocletian's son in-law, and Constantius (surnamed Chlorus—'the pale') were made deputy emperors with the title of Caesar. Galerius was given authority over the Danube provinces and Dalmatia, while Constantius took over Britain, Gaul and Spain. Significantly, Diocletian retained all his eastern provinces and set up his regional headquarters at Nicomedia in Bithynia, where he held court with all the outward show of an eastern potentate, complete with regal trappings and elaborate ceremonial.[2]

So we can clearly see from the above that the system of leadership in the empire had declined since the days of Caesar. So here is what we should have learned in this section: nowhere does the Scripture say the toes are ten in number. As we look at the image in Daniel 2:31–33, it included pictures of the four beasts. Moving from the top of it toward the bottom we have: Babylon (the head) at the top, then Medo-Persia (the upper part of the shoulders and the chest), followed by Greece (the middle portion of the image's body), and the last being the Roman Empire, which was seen on the image (from the hips, down the legs, and to the feet with the toes). There are only four beasts shown on or in the image, and they all came to their end at different times throughout history. Nowhere is there a revival of the fourth beast represented by ten toes, but there will be a revival of all four beasts, and they will play a very important part during the tribulation period and will be in power *together* during that time, and all four will be destroyed simultaneously. We will see this in Daniel 2:33–35 in chapter 6 of this book.

Third False Teaching: *The ten horns in Daniel 7 are the same ten horns in Revelation 17.*

We have been taught that the ten horns of both chapters are the *same,* and they are *not.* This is false teaching, and we'll see it as such when we compare both sets of horns in the following Scriptures. We'll start in Daniel 7 first: In Daniel 7:17, an angel had just told Daniel, **"These great beasts, which are four kings** (kingdoms), **which shall arise out of the earth."** This is also seen in verses 3 through 14 of the same chapter. Daniel was very concerned about the fourth beast and wanted to know the truth about it in verse 19, **"Then I would know the truth of the fourth beast . . ."** Now pay close attention to verse 20: **"And of the ten horns that were in his head, and of the other which came up, and before whom three fell . . ."** This interpretation agrees with what was said in verse 8 of the same chapter.

Notice two things that are very important. *First,* the ten kings were already in existence when the little horn comes up among them, and *second*, three of the horns are plucked up by their roots or fall in verse 20. These verses tell us that these three kings are *no more!* We will cover the identity of the little horn later in this book. Now, let's go to Revelation 17 so that we can compare the ten horns mentioned there to these in Daniel 7. John, in Revelation 17:3, writes, **"We see a beast in the wilderness which has a woman sitting on it, and the beast has seven heads, and ten horns."** Now let's proceed to verse 12: **"And the ten horns which thou sawest are ten kings, which have received no kingdom as yet: but receive power as kings one hour with the beast."**

First, we need to notice that the ten kings do not have a kingdom yet, but when the Antichrist crowns them as ten, watch what happens. Revelation 17:12 says, **"And the ten kings which thou sawest are ten kings, which have received no kingdom as yet; but receive power as kings one hour with the beast** [the Antichrist].**"** Remember, all of Revelation 17 is symbolism, so don't take this one hour literally. It most likely means a short period of time. Unlike the horns of Daniel 7, who already existed in their kingly positions when the little horn comes up *after* they are kings, Revelation 17:16–17 will show us that these kings are different: **"And the ten kings which thou sawest upon the beast, these shall hate the whore** [false church] . . .**"** They'll destroy the harlot, which is the false church, and when we look at the rest of the next verse, 17, it will show us why these ten horns are different than those in Daniel 7.

Look at what the Scripture says about these ten kings. Revelation 17:17 says, **"For God hath put in their hearts to fulfill his will, and to agree, and give their kingdom unto the beast, until the words of God shall be fulfilled."** Notice that these kings, unlike those mentioned in Daniel 7, never become seven in number. They start as *ten*, and *remain ten until* the Word of our Lord is *fulfilled*. So we see a totally different set of ten horns in Revelation 17 than those of Daniel 7. When we get to the next chapter, we will discover not only who the little horn is, but we will also find out through the Scriptures more evidence of who the 10-3=7 horns are.

It is very obvious that these two sets of horns (kings) are different, yet many a teacher I have sat under taught that they were the same by pulling them out of context. For example, a well-known TV prophecy teacher taught that the ten horns of Daniel 10:20 are ten of the coming kings of the European common market nations that will be under the authority of the Antichrist, who will remove three of them, and thus they become seven. This is a prime example of studying the scriptures using the eisegesis method, which is reading into the text what a person thinks it says, and that is how we have believed this false teaching of those ten horns being the same. If we fail to study the scriptures ourselves and believe what the teachers of prophecy have taught us, then we have no one to blame but ourselves.

Fourth False Teaching: *The stone cut without hands in Daniel 2 is Christ.*

We have been taught this by every preacher, writer of prophecy, and TV prophecy program that I can remember. They have taught us in Daniel 1:45 that Christ is the rock that will break in pieces, the image that represents the human governments, and put them to their end and bring in his kingdom. Here is the problem with that interpretation: the word used for stone in Daniel 2:45 is *eben*, and it means, **"A small part, sliver, to build, or diver's weight."** Compare that with the word rock used in Exodus 17:6, **"And thou shall smite the *rock* . . ."** We have been taught in this text that the word rock represents our Lord, and in the Hebrew language the word used for rock is *tsur,* which means, "A rock, mighty one, God rock, strong, and strength," and what a contrast this is to the word used in Daniel 2:45.

Now let's back up one verse to 44b, **"And the kingdom shall not be left to other people, but *it* shall break in pieces and consume all these kingdoms, and *it* shall stand forever."** And again in verse 45 it says, **"The stone was cut of the *mountain* without hands, and that *it* brake in pieces . . ."** Remember the previous teaching on the word *mountains*, meaning *nations*? So the above verse means the stone was cut out of the nations. Also,

God has never been known or described as "it," for he is referred to as him, his, I am, he, God, and Lord. The gender of the noun "it" in Daniel 2:44 is neuter, which means a thing, and thus it can't be a person. What we see here in Daniel is that in the last days, our Lord will begin with a small portion of a nation, seen as a stone, back again in the land where there was once a full twelve tribes of people filling the land and known as his holy mountain.

This stone that was cut out of the mountain "without hands" took place in 1948 when the United Nations gave the Jewish people a small portion of land in Israel without them having to fight for it, and truly the hand of God, not human hands, was controlling the whole situation. After the gentile nations are judged and brought low, this nation will grow into a large or high mountain that will rule the world. God will use that small stone during the tribulation period to bring judgment to the nations. In Jeremiah 50–51, the destruction of end-time Babylon is covered, which takes place during the tribulation period. Look at Jeremiah 51:19–23, **"The portion of Jacob** (Israel) **is not like them."** I will stop here for a moment to point out two words: Jacob, which means Israel, and the word portion, which means *a part*, or *part*, but *not all*. This is the stone of Daniel 2.

Now let's look at the rest of the text to see if God uses them to break the nations in pieces by picking up where we left off: **"For he is the former of all things: and Israel is the rod of his inheritance: the Lord of Hosts is his name . . . Thou art my battle axe and the weapons of war: for with thee will I break in pieces the nations, and with thee will I destroy kingdoms."** As you read on through verses 21 to 23, you'll see God breaking everything with the nation of Israel. Take a look at another text in Zechariah 12:3, **"And in that day will I make Jerusalem a burdensome *stone* for all people: all that burden themselves with it** [the stone] **shall be cut in pieces, though all the peoples of the earth be gathered together against it."** Our Lord will use Israel to judge the nations. Look at Zechariah 14:1–3, **"Behold, the day of the Lord cometh, and thy spoil shall be divided in the midst of thee. For I will gather *all* nations against Jerusalem to battle; and the city shall be taken, and the houses rifled** [plundered]**, and the women** ravished; and half the city shall go forth into captivity, and the residue of the people shall not be cut off from the city." **"Then shall the Lord go forth, and** *fight against those nations*, **as when he fought in the day of battle."**

In Ezekiel 38:1–4, we see more proof, **"I will turn thee back and put hooks into thy jaws, and I will bring thee forth . . ."** Here our Lord is bringing Russia and her allies against his stone (small nation) in the latter days. Verse 8 says, **"After many days thou shalt be visited: in the latter years."** A multitude of them shall come. Verse 9b continues, **"Thou shalt be like a cloud to cover the land, thou and all thy bands** (troops), **and many people with thee,"** so that the Lord can destroy them and be glorified by the Jews after destroying almost all of this mass of people. Verse 23 says, **"Thus will I magnify myself, and sanctify myself, and I will be known in the eyes of many nations, and they shall know that I am the Lord."**

Back on August 5, 2006, Israel was at war in Lebanon with the Hezbollah terrorists, and she was adding enemies daily as the war went on. Only the true believer can see the hand of God with that nation today, but during the tribulation period, many nations, meaning nationalities, will come to know the Lord. Today's Christians should be excited about the signs of the times that we are seeing as they point to the soon coming of our Lord Jesus Christ for his church. The Lord is working with this "partial people nation" to bring others against it, so that he can judge them. It is what God has planned to do from the beginning of time for the judgment to come during the last days, according to the Old Testament prophets.

The last war will take place at the end of the tribulation period in Revelation 16:12–14 at the pouring out of the sixth angel, our Lord allowing frogs (demon spirits) to go out to the kings of the world to give them the idea of gathering together to do battle against God's people Israel at Armageddon. It's really amazing when we think about the future of Israel and how our Lord will use that small nation, with just a few of her people, to bring an end to the gentile nations that have ruled the world under Satan for almost six thousand years. So the true teaching of what, or who, the stone is, *is Israel*. Just a reminder from an earlier study in this book: Israel, the stone, becomes a mountain and fills the whole earth.

Thus the *eben* stone of Daniel 2 is not Christ, as we have been taught, but Israel, which is still a stone today and will grow into a mountain that will fill the whole earth, just as God promised King David. Please excuse this weak analogy of the Lord using Israel to judge the nations: it's like God bowling, with Israel as the bowling ball, knocking down the pins, which are the nations, while remembering the force or power behind the ball is God. Thus he gets the glory for everything that happens during the tribulation period.

Fifth False Teaching: *The little horn of Daniel 7 is the Antichrist.*

This false teaching has been taken from Daniel 2, 7–8. As we study these chapters, we need to remember this: each chapter progressively reveals more than the chapter preceding it does. In other words, we cannot get all of the necessary information from one chapter to correctly interpret it and get a clear picture of what the three chapters are teaching us.

Let's start in Daniel 7:2–8, and without quoting any of it but explaining it as it reveals the four beasts to us. In verse 2, Daniel has a dream about four great beasts that **"came up from the sea"** in verse 3. Since this is a symbolic text, the word for sea doesn't mean the ocean or rivers, so it must be given a figurative interpretation, and it most likely represents the sea of nations or people. Then Daniel goes on to describe each beast, with verse 4 containing the first beast, verse 5 the second beast, verse 6 the third beast, and verses 7 and 8 revealing to us the fourth beast. The error of past and present authors, and today's pastor/teachers, is their assumption that the ten horns of verses 7 and 8 are the same ten horns of the Antichrist's beast kingdom seen in Revelation 17, but notice in verse 8, the little horn sets aside three of the horns (kings), and in Revelation 17:16–17, the ten horns of the beast's government system are always ten in number, even until the Word of God is fulfilled. We covered this in the teaching in chapter 4.

Many of the teachers of prophecy have also taught us that the little horn is the Antichrist in this text. This is caused by reading into the text without giving a serious account to what the rest of the chapter says. We must always take out what is in the Scriptures. We can interpret it correctly only when we have compared it to the surrounding verses, and other books of the Bible where these horns are mentioned, and then with much prayer and study, followed with a lot of patience while waiting upon the Lord to reveal the correct interpretation of this text. First we need to see that there are only four beasts mentioned in this text, and the fourth one has the ten horns. To see where these ten horns are placed, we need to jump ahead to verses 16 through 26, where in verse 16 it says an angel begins to tell Daniel the interpretation of his dream. In verse 17, we see the number of the beasts is *four*, and in verses 19 and 20, we see the placement of the ten horns, which are *in* the *head* of the *fourth beast*, and the little horn comes up and displaces *three* of the horns.

One thing is certain: they all belong to the same empire, nation, or city, as the ten were in the head of the fourth beast, which is the Roman Empire of the past, and the little horn comes up among them. The horns were not placed on the fourth head but were already in it. I cannot find a place in the Scriptures where the Antichrist or his kingdom, both known as the beast, is described as a single horn at any time. In Revelation 17:9–12, we see the eighth head having ten horns that will be crowned, and once again in verse 17, the ten horns stay that number *until* the Word of God is fulfilled.

I believe that the little horn of Daniel 7 is called the little horn because he represents a little nation with a big voice of influence in this world and has since the breakup of the Roman Empire. I believe that the little horn represents the false church in the world, which has been headed up by the popes of the Roman Catholic Church. The ten horns represent the last of the kings of the divided Roman Empire and the two legs of that empire after it split up, and the two legs are the eastern and western branches. The only kingdom that came out of the old Roman Empire and still exists today is the kingdom of Vatican City with its popes. It has its own government, prints and makes its own money, and has power over the vast majority of what is called Christendom today, and with this power and influence, it will be the head of the false church in the first three and one half years of the tribulation period.

Now let's go back to the little horn of Daniel 7, and we will see further proof that this horn is not the Antichrist. We are going to compare the two persons: the little horn of Daniel 7, with the **"king of fierce countenance,"** seen here in Daniel 8:23–25. Let's examine how this little horn's kingdom will come to an end. According to verse 25 of Daniel 7, this little horn has power to change times and laws and speak against the Most High, **"until a time, and times, and the dividing of time,"** translated as one year, two years, and a half of a year, or three and a half years. He will have a dominion (religious in nature) for the first three and a half years of Daniel's seventieth week while the Antichrist is busy bringing all the nations together through his peaceful effort.

Let me explain Daniel's seventieth week: it is a week of seven years that takes place just before the return of Jesus Christ to Earth. The last three and a half years of the seven years are known as the *great tribulation period* or the time of God's judgment on the nations. When the person known as the little horn comes to the middle of Daniel's seventieth week, he loses his dominion, which is seen in verse 26, **"*They* shall take away his dominion, to consume and destroy it unto the end."** Who are the *"they"* of verse 26? Go to Revelation 17:16 for the answer, **"And the ten horns which thou sawest upon the beast, *these* shall hate the whore** [false religious system, or world church of the first half of Daniel's seventieth week] **and shall make her desolate and naked, and shall eat her flesh, and burn her with fire."**

Now notice the word these in verse 16, the *"these"* of this text are the "they" of the text in Daniel 7. Also notice that there is no mention of the little horn's end but just his dominion. He most likely is the person who becomes the second beast of Revelation 13:11–18, known as the false prophet, who will direct all the people he had dominion over in the first half of the tribulation period to worship the first beast of Revelation 13:1–10 known as the Antichrist. I have found nothing else from Scripture to support the possibility of this little horn of Daniel 7 being the Antichrist.

Now let's look at the person in Daniel 8 known as the *"king of fierce countenance"* for the purpose of comparing him to the little horn of chapter 7. Starting in Daniel 8:23–24, **"And in the latter time of their kingdom** [the kingdom of the four beasts], **when the transgressors are to come to the full** [their fullness], **a king of fierce countenance, and understanding dark sentences, shall stand up. And his power shall be mighty, but not by his own power . . ."** This is the Antichrist, as we know that he is *empowered* by *Satan*, who is cast out of heaven in the middle of the seven years, or the last week of seven years that God deals with the restoration of the nation of Israel. He also destroys **"the mighty and the holy people,"** as it says in the end of this verse.

Now here is the proof that the little horn of chapter seven is not the Antichrist, and this person in chapter 8 is. Verse 25b says, **"And he shall magnify himself in his heart** [he says that he is God, and demands the worship of all the people dwelling on planet Earth] **and by peace shall destroy many: he shall also stand up against the Prince of princes** [the Lord Jesus Christ]**; but he shall be broken without hand."** For added proof from another text that agrees with this verse where it says he comes to *his end without hand*, turn to 2 Thessalonians 2:3–8. In verses 3–4, it says, **"And that man of sin be revealed, the son of perdition who opposeth and exalteth himself above all that is called God, or that is worshipped; so that he as God sitteth in the temple of God, showing himself that he is God."**

This is the Antichrist claiming he is God, and we see *him* as a *person*, coming to an *end*, not just *his dominion*, like that of the little horn in chapter 7 of the book of Daniel. **"And then** [after the Holy Spirit is taken out of the way in the preceding verse] **shall that wicked one be revealed whom the Lord shall consume with the spirit of his mouth, and shall destroy with the**

brightness of his coming." The Lord destroys him by himself, without any human hands involved. Notice the differences between the two persons of Daniel chapter 7 and 8, and let's see the contrast between these two people:

1. The person in Daniel 7 lost his dominion through a group mentioned as *they.*
2. The person in 2 Thessalonians 8 was consumed *by the Lord.*
3. The person in Daniel 7 has his dominion was taken away by people.
4. The person in 2 Thessalonians 8 was broken without hand.
5. The person in Daniel 7 had a three-and-a-half year dominion.
6. The person in 2 Thessalonians 8 is the Antichrist, and he has a seven-year reign, as we know from other Scriptures in the Bible. He reigns during the first three and a half years with peace, and then the last three and a half years with force while demanding the people to worship him as God during the time of Jacob's (meaning Israel's) trouble, which is also known as the great tribulation period.

Before closing this section on the little horn of Daniel 7, I would like to make some more comments on the four beasts seen in both chapters 7 and 8 from the Scriptures in the book of Daniel. These are not only a picture of past kingdoms that existed chronologically as proven by history past that was witnessed over the last twenty-six hundred years. I have been taught this truth by every teacher I've listened to in the past thirty-two years, but I have never been taught that the four beasts of the image will all be in existence again at the same time as nations and be part of the ruling kingdoms of the last world government system and will all exist simultaneously during the tribulation period. That's correct, as all these—Babylon, represented by a mighty end time nation, Medes, represented as Iran, Greece, as Greece, and Rome, represented by the European common market—will be resurrected together with the shaky legs and toes of iron and clay at the bottom of the image again, and they will all topple together, as the Scripture says in Daniel 2:35.

Speaking of the four beasts, Daniel says in 2:32–33, 35, **"This image's head was of fine gold, his breast, and arms of silver, his belly and his thighs of brass, his legs of iron, his feet part of iron and part of clay . . . Then was the iron, the clay, the brass, the silver, and the gold, broken to pieces *together.*"** The stone that the Lord uses to topple them is Israel, and that stone will become a great mountain (world kingdom) that will replace those kingdoms of men, including the last world government system of mankind that will exist during the tribulation period and fill the whole earth. This stone is seen in verses thirty four and thirty five of Daniel 2. How does this compare with what we have been taught? We have erroneously been taught that the ten toes of the image will be resurrected to be and represent the revived Roman Empire, and along with the Antichrist ruling them, they will represent and be the beast that will rule the world during the tribulation period.

In closing this part of the study, let me cover another misinterpretation that our end-time authors and teachers have taught us. Some of them have said that the Antichrist will come out of Rome or from Europe or one of its nations. They use Daniel 9:26 as the proof of this teaching, **"And after threescore and two weeks shall Messiah be cut off,** [the death of Jesus] **but not for himself and the people of the prince that shall come** [AD 70 Titus and the Romans that destroyed Jerusalem] **shall destroy the city and the sanctuary . . ."** Now let's open our minds just a little bit to realize that the seed of the people that lived in the Roman Empire, or Rome itself, in AD 70 have *by the millions* over the last two thousand years moved to other nations around the world, and most of them can be found in the United States. So when the scriptures say the people of the prince (Antichrist), it means that he will come from the seed of the old Roman Empire people, not necessarily Rome located in Italy. Today, if all the people would move out of Rome, then Rome would not be a city with a civil government, and the buildings would only remind us where it once existed as a city. Since the people are what make up a city, and many people, being of the seed of the old Roman

Empire, have moved to many other nations, then this person called the Antichrist can come from just about any nation on this planet.

We will see in the final chapter of this book the nation where the Antichrist will rule from. Scripture from Isaiah 14 will reveal the nation he rules from.

Chapter 4

Why the Church Is Unaware of
These False Doctrines

The Bible tells us in Revelation 3:14–22 that the church of today is called the Laodicean church. We are going to take a close look at this church and its spiritual condition. Revelation 3:14 says, **"And unto the angel of *the church* of the Laodiceans write; These things saith the Amen, the faithful and true witness, the beginning of the creation of God."** Our Lord is talking to born-again Christians who are not in fellowship with him, and we need to see that this is true. We'll do so by keeping this verse in the context with the surrounding verses. These Christians are not losing their salvation by his spewing them out of his mouth. We need to notice that our Lord Jesus Christ is having the apostle John write this to the angel (messenger) of his church. So, because of this, we can rule out the fact that this Scripture is *not* being directed to the unsaved or lost people who are just religious.

In verses 15 and 16, he says, **"I know thy works, that thou art neither cold nor hot; I would** "wish" **thou wert** "were" **cold or hot. So then because thou art lukewarm, and neither cold nor hot, I will spew thee out of my mouth."** Take a quick look at verse 20 of the text to see what Jesus is talking about. **"Behold,**

I stand at the door, and knock: if any man [male or female] **hear my voice, and open the door, I will come into him, and I will sup** [have fellowship] **with him, and he with me."** These are Christians who are out of fellowship with the Lord, and they are blind to it, because their sin is hard to be seen by them. It is the sin of ruling or controlling their lives and not seeking the will of God daily. It also is the sin of not following or putting into practice the total Word of God. Keeping God's Word means more than just living a good, moral life and attending worship services. These people attend church up to two or three times a week, and they are good, moral people. The message, or subject of this text, is similar to that of John 15, and both it and this text show us a major problem that the current-day Laodicean church has.

John 15:5–6 says, **"I am the true vine, ye are the branches: He that abideth** [stays in fellowship] **in me, and *I in* him, the same bringeth forth much fruit: for without me you can do nothing. If a man abideth not in me, he is cast forth as a branch, and he is withered, and men gather them, and cast them into the fire, and they are burned."** In other words, there will be no fruit (good works) on their branches that have been burned up. It sounds like these Christians are being cast into hell, but they aren't! It is their works, or lack thereof, that they have performed in the flesh (sinful nature) all by themselves, without any leading of the Holy Spirit that are burning up. Compare these verses with 1 Corinthians 3:13–15, **"Every man's** [Christians in this text] **work shall be made manifest: for the day shall declare it, because it shall be revealed by fire, and the fire shall try everyman's work of what sort it is. If any man's work abide which he hath built thereupon, he shall receive a reward. If any man's work shall be burned, he shall suffer loss; but he himself shall be saved; yet so as by fire."** Fire will not destroy the salvation of the believer, because the blood of our Lord Jesus Christ that saved us from our sins is greater than fire!

When a believer is not in fellowship with the Lord, he will not be involved in a ministry that has been motivated by the indwelling Spirit of God. We as believers make choices. First we can make the choice of not getting involved in a ministry for the

Lord. Second we can make a choice of doing something for him that we like to do. The latter choice is the one that a Christian makes that causes him/her to lose fellowship with the Lord. They satisfy their sinful natures, and they will not produce any fruit. The next choice is the only choice that will bear any fruit, and it is to walk (have fellowship) with the Lord daily and allow him to direct our lives by using our God-given gifts in a God-given ministry, as he told them in John 15:5, at the end of the verse, **"For without me you can do nothing."**

So what is the Lord saying in Revelation 3:16, **"I will spew you out of my mouth"**? He is saying this to the vast majority of his end-time church, known as the Laodicean portion of it today. No wonder our Lord said in Luke 18:8, **"Nevertheless when the Son of man cometh, shall he find faith on the earth?"** In other words, our Lord was saying, "When I return, will I find my people living by faith?" Now it's one thing to be saved by faith and another thing to live by it. In Romans 10:17, we see where faith comes from, **"So then faith cometh by hearing, and hearing by the word of God."** The apostle Paul wrote to Timothy in 2 Timothy 3:14–17, **"But continue thou in the things which thou hast learned and hast been assured of, knowing of whom thou hast learned them. And that from a child thou hast known the holy Scriptures, which are able to make thee wise unto salvation through faith which is in Christ Jesus."** As a young boy, Timothy was taught the Word of God, and Paul is admonishing him to continue in the things that he had been taught from the Word of God. That is what faith is all about!

Brothers and sisters in Christ, there is a great difference between listening to your pastor preach or teach the Word of God on Sunday morning and you hearing it *from the Lord* and applying it your life by faith. I'm not saying that we won't fail from time to time, but are you hearing a message from the Lord and ignoring it, or are you applying it to your life by faith? This chapter is not being written to the believers who have sinned and repented to walk with the Lord again but to the Christians who cannot see their sins because of the "spiritual sleeping condition" they are currently in, and these are the Christians who are not in fellowship with the Lord. They are also the people mentioned in Revelation 3 as neither cold nor hot. They are similar to the Hebrew children who refused to obey God in the day of provocation mentioned in Numbers 14. Because of their rebellion (not believing and trusting the Lord), God took them all home (through death) in the next forty years. We are talking about at least a million people in Numbers 14.

Now what I'm about to say may be hard to believe and understand. These Christians mentioned in Revelation 3 could be, when comparing it with what the Lord did in the day of provocation, spewed out of his mouth at his coming (rapture of the church) and left behind to go through that terrible time. I say this and back it with the Scripture as seen in Revelation 3:8, 10, where our Lord says to the other portion of believers in his church of the end time that has kept his word. Revelation 3:8, 10 says, **"I know thy works: behold** [look at, regard] **I have set before thee an open door, and no man can shut it: for thou hast little strength, and has kept my word, and hast not denied my name . . . Because thou hast kept the word of my patience, I will** [promise to these only] **keep thee from the hour** [time] **of temptation, which shall try them that dwell upon the earth."** This is the portion of his end-time church that is keeping his word and looking for his coming. They will be kept out of the tribulation period, says the Lord to them, but notice that there is no promise like that to the Laodicean Church. Only to them that repent in that church is there any hope of missing it.

I'm not 100 percent sure of what I'm about to say, but it may be the our Lord is teaching us that there is a partial rapture about to take place where some believers are taken and the balance are left behind to go through the last three and a half years that will be the time known as Daniel's trouble, or the time of the judgment of God, that will come upon all the earth. You say, "He wouldn't do that to his church." Well, he did it to the believers who wouldn't obey him in the Old Testament. And our Bible tells us, **"Jesus Christ the same yesterday, and today, and for ever"** (Heb. 13:8). Take this as a warning to get right with the Lord and fellowship with him daily, and we won't have to be concerned about missing his best for us. There is a warning for anyone who is currently in this Laodicean church, and it is seen in Revelation 3:21–22, **"To him that overcometh will I grant to sit with me in my throne, even as I also overcame, and am set down with my Father in his throne. He that hath an ear, let him *hear* what *the Spirit* saith unto the churches."**

The Lord, through his Holy Spirit, our teacher, is saying if you are in a spiritual slumber, it's time to repent and wake up. Allow him to guide you daily to find your God-given gift, and use it to glorify him in the body of Christ. Get into the Word of God and study it so you can check out any man who teaches you any Scripture from the Bible, to the place where you can rightly divide it, and find out whether you have been taught it as false doctrine or correct. That is a responsibility you have to God, so do it

We live in a day when there are very few pastors who actually teach us the Scriptures line by line, word to word, through several verses in one text.

I visited a church in Columbia, South Carolina, last year, and the pastor only used one verse of Scripture for his whole sermon, and that verse was taught incorrectly because he pulled it out of context. I will never go back to hear him speak again! I tried to teach a Christian about the contents of my book, and she attacked me verbally and said, "So what? You believe it one way and others believe it differently." They will not listen to sound doctrine, and they do not want to. They have been taught one way, and they'll stick with that teaching, and they don't want to hear the truth, because they believe they have it already. It's a sad day when Christians close their ears to the truth!

There are other churches that exist under Christian names but do not know Christ at all. They have mastered religious ritual and know about Jesus Christ but don't have him as a personal Savior. They follow religion without relationship, and it is relationship that God wants with them on a personal basis. They do many works under the name of Jesus Christ, and they are the people he is addressing in Matthew 7:21–23, **"Not every one that saith unto me, Lord, Lord, shall enter the kingdom of heaven. *Many* will say to me in that day, Lord, Lord, have**

we not prophesied in thy name? and in thy name have cast out devils [demons]**? And in thy name done many wonderful works? And I will profess unto them, I never *knew* you: depart from me, ye that work iniquity."** He never knew them, because they had no personal relationship with him. They just practiced a religious ritual under the name of a Christian church.

Chapter 5

End-Time Babylon Revealed

Some of this study will be repetitive with chapter 2 in this book. In the Scripture, there are four distinct Babylons mentioned, with the first being that of the *tower* Babel, the second one is the *city* of ancient Babylon, which is located in Iraq, third, there is *religious* Babylon, and last, there is *commercial* Babylon, which is a *country* in existence during the end times. This country is in existence today, and this study will center on the latter of the four, which can be titled commercial, political, or end-time Babylon. When the words *end times* are used, they do not mean the end of the world but the end of human government systems that are ruling the world, just before the return of Jesus Christ to the earth.

The two primary chapters in the book of Revelation that we will study in this chapter are 17 and 18. John is told us in Revelation 17:7, **"The mystery of the woman, and the beast that carrieth her which hath seven heads and ten horns."** Here we see Ecclesiastical (religious) Babylon in the person of a woman who is riding the beast. In Revelation 18, we see commercial Babylon identified as a civil authority or a nation. There is no specific mention of her location, but there are several characteristics about her that help us in understanding who she most likely is. The Word of God identifies Babylon by the feminine pronouns: her and she throughout this entire chapter. Whoever she is, she will be totally annihilated before the end of the great tribulation period. We will look at other books and their chapters in the Bible to help us identify who Commercial Babylon is:

1. Isaiah 13, 14, 18, 47
2. Jeremiah 50, 51
3. Revelation 13, 17, 18
4. Daniel 7, 8

Understanding who the main players are is essential if you are to come to any truth of Bible prophecy concerning the end times and why world events are happening as they are. Jesus warned us that deception is the key to the rising of the Antichrist. That means he comes to power in a place not recognized and at a time we aren't expecting him. The vast majority of God's people, let alone the world at large, are being deceived, and they are not aware of it. The prophetic world today is in deep delusion, and they are looking in the wrong area for the rise of the antichrist forces and Lucifer.

Whenever we look at a text in the Bible concerning Babylon, we need to determine whether the writer is talking about Babylon past, present, or future, and we need to do that from the viewpoint of the writer's day being present-day Babylon. It's fairly easy to determine which Babylon the writer is talking about by examining what is being said about the nation in the surrounding verses. For example, let's look at Jeremiah 50:1–4, **"The word that the Lord spake against Babylon and against the land of the Chaldeans by Jeremiah the prophet. Declare ye among the nations, and publish, and conceal not: say, Babylon is taken, Bel is confounded . . ."** First, let's answer this question: who are the Chaldeans? Here is the answer to taken from, *Arbatel of Magic*, translated into English by Robert Turner, London 1655:[5]

> When the wise men came to worship Jesus, and this is the first and highest kind, which is called divine Magick; and these the Latins did entitle *sapientes,* or wise men: for the fear and worship of God, is the beginning of knowledge. These wise men the Greeks call *Philosophers;* and amongst the Egyptians they were termed *Priests;* the Hebrews termed them *Cabalistos,* Prophets, Scribes and Pharisees; and amongst the Babylonians they were differenced by the name of *Chaldeans;* & by the Persians they were called *Magicians.*

So modern-day Babylon is also the place, known as it was in ancient time, as the Land of the Chaldeans, or the place where most of the modern-day philosophers, wise men, and magicians dwell. The question is: how do we know whether the Babylon mentioned in Jeremiah 50 is before, during, or after Jeremiah's time? The answer is found in Jeremiah 50:2–4, where it says, **"In those days, the days of Babylon being taken, and her land becoming desolate . . . and in that time, saith the Lord, the children of Israel shall come, they and the children of Judah** [key word follows] *together*, **going and weeping: they shall go, and seek the Lord their God. In those days . . ."** What days? The answer is in verse two, **"Babylon is taken, Bel is confounded, Merodach is broken in pieces: her idols are confounded, her images are broken in pieces."** Here we see Babylon being destroyed with her gods, and verse 4 gives us the time frame that this will take place in: **"In those days and in that time, saith the Lord, the children of Israel shall come, they and the children of Judah together, going and weeping: they shall go, and seek the Lord their God."** These are the believers, both Jew and tribulation saints who were told to come out of her in Revelation 18:4. A further explanation of this is wherever Babylon is located, it contains a lot of Jewish people and will have many tribulation believers in her just before God destroys her.

Now, what I am about to say might be very hard to understand, because we have been taught that the Samaritans in the land of Israel when Jesus was here were a result of the intermixing of Jews and gentiles, which is not true at all. Notice in verse 4 where it says, **"The children of Israel shall; come, they and the children of Judah together . . ."** We see *two* distinct groups of people here:

1. The children of Israel
2. The children of Judah.

I don't have the time in this study to cover in detail the complete biblical record of these nations, but I will tell you that most of the Old Testament Scriptures contain the history of these two nations. Briefly, it is as follows. After Solomon was the king over all of Israel—all twelve tribes—the nation split into two kingdoms. The northern portion had ten of the tribes and the southern had two tribes, the tribe of Judah and the tribe of Benjamin, along with some of the priests from the tribe of the Levites and their families. Both nations had their own kings, and while Judah and Benjamin worshiped the Lord correctly, according the way the Lord had set it up, the northern kingdom became imbedded with their idols. Second Chronicles 11:3 says, **"Speak to Rehoboam the son of Solomon, king of Judah, and to all Israel in Judah and Benjamin, saying, Thus saith the Lord, Ye shall not go up, nor fight against your brethren . . ."** We can see that clearly by what was just said by the Lord in this verse. In 1 Kings 12:28, we see the problem and sin of the northern tribes, **"Whereupon the king** [evil king Jeroboam of the northern kingdom] **took counsel, and made two calves of gold, and said unto them, It is too much for you to go up to Jerusalem: behold thy gods, O Israel, which brought thee up out of the land of Egypt. And he set the one in Bethel, and the other put he in Dan."**

Notice that the king of the northern tribes said that to worship in Jerusalem would be to go up, even though they were above Jerusalem geographically. Whenever our worship is toward God, the direction is always up. The northern tribes elected to worship in another direction opposite that of Judah and Benjamin. We need to know this very important fact if we expect to rightly divide God's Word: God sent his prophets to warn the northern tribes of his coming judgment, but they listened not, killed many of his prophets, and continued their ungodly practices. Finally, in 722 BC, the Lord brought the Assyrians against the northern kingdom, and drove them out of the land. Second Kings 17:5–6, 18 says, **"Therefore the Lord was very angry with Israel, and removed them out of His sight: there was *none left* but the tribe of *Judah only.*"** The northern kingdom was completely removed out of the land! Even though the Scripture says Judah only, that tribe is seen some two hundred plus years later, when they came out of captivity from Babylon, as mentioned in Ezra 4:1, **"Now when the adversaries of Judah and Benjamin . . ."**

You can see that Benjamin is said to be with Judah. The answer to this is that the tribe of Benjamin, which was located next to the tribe of Judah in southern Israel, practiced Judaism, which made them Jews. The Lord removed some of the tribe of Benjamin, which had gone astray with the other tribes. Again, we must know this very important fact if we expect to rightly divide God's Word: *Judah* means *Jews*, and the northern tribes, even though they, like Judah, had received the instructions from the Lord on how they were to worship, refused to worship as Jews. When they were taken captive by the Assyrians, the Israelites of the northern kingdom were mixed in with the gentiles of Assyria and several other nations they had escaped to. Those who were captured were removed from the land and have not returned to Israel, even to this very day.

Now the question is: where are the northern tribes today? They are mixed in with the gentiles and living in many of today's nations where God scattered them to. We can't identify them, but God knows every one of them, what seed or tribe that they came from, and where they live. The Jews, and especially Orthodox Jews, are more identifiable due to the fact that they have, for the most part, kept themselves separate from mixing with other races by marrying within their own race and have kept many of the customs of the religion. You might be saying, "But what about the Samaritans who were in the land when Jesus walked the earth?" Second Kings 17:24 says, **"And the king of Assyria brought men from Babylon, and Cuthah, and from Ava, and**

from Sepharvaim, and placed them in the cities of Samaria instead of the children of Israel: and they possessed Samaria, and dwelt in the cities thereof."

We have been taught that the Samaritans of Jesus day were half-Jew and half-gentile, which is another false teaching that has been passed down to us by teachers and pastors who failed to dig into the Scriptures. The Scripture says they were gentiles who were placed in the land and taught the things of the God of the land (Israel). See 2 Kings 17:26-28, where it says the people that were brought into the land by the Assyrian king. Verse 26 says they **"knew not the manner of the God of the land,"** so one of the Levite priests was sent to them to instruct them in the way, as seen in verses 27 and 28. All Jews are Israelites, but all Israelites are not Jews. If anyone is willing to spend some time studying the Old Testament, he or she will find this to be very true.

Here are just two more verses to prove the point above about the fact that not all Israelites are Jews. Jerusalem, where Judah existed, was about to be attacked by two kings: one from Syria, and the other the son of Remaliah, king of Israel (the northern kingdom). Second Kings 16:5-6 says, **"Then Rezin king of Syria, and Pekah son of Remaliah king of Israel came up to Jerusalem to war; and they besieged *Ahaz*, but could not overcome him. At the time Rezin king of Syria recovered Elath to Syria, and drove *the Jews* from Elath . . ."**

Here we see two nations: *Israel*, in this text, meaning the *northern tribes*, and Syria battling King Ahaz, king of *Judah*, which means *Jews*. Notice in verse 6 that they drove the Jews out of Elath. We see here that the only kingdom called the Jews was the southern kingdom. The northern kingdom, who were the children of Abraham as well as the tribes of Judah and Benjamin, were rebels who refused to follow the God-instructed way of worship, which was to take place in Jerusalem through the tribe of Judah. Another place in Scripture that supports the teaching of two houses of Israel is seen in Isaiah 8:14, **"But for a stone of stumbling and for a rock of offense to *both* houses of Israel . . ."** The two kingdoms have been separated since 722 BC, and only a portion of the nation of Judah, which included the

47

tribe of Benjamin, is back in the land today. Our Lord is going to bring many of the seeds of the north and some more of the Jews that were scattered in other nations back during the tribulation period.

Another proof of the two nations coming back is seen in Ezekiel 37, which is titled as the *Valley of the Dry Bones*. We see in this chapter the restoration of the two nations, which will be united as one again. In the first eleven verses, we see a picture of "the whole house of Israel" being spiritually dead. Go forward to verse 16, which says, **"Moreover, thou son of man, take thee one stick, and write on it, For Judah, and for the children of Israel his companions: then take another stick, and write upon it, For Joseph, the stick of Ephraim, and for all the house of Israel his companions."** It's easy to see that there are two sticks for the whole house of Israel. Read verses 17 through 24 and you'll see further proof that the two nations of Israel will become one again. Verse 22b says, **"And one king shall be king to them all; and they shall be no more two nations, neither shall they be divided into two kingdoms any more at all."** Verse 24 says, **"And David my servant shall be king over them . . ."** This text supports the two kingdoms returning together during the end times in Jeremiah chapters 50 and 51, along with Isaiah 13 and 14.

Now let's go back and pick up where we left off. In the text, Jeremiah 50:4, when it said the Israelites and the Jews would be seeking God together at or near the end-time, Babylon will be destroyed. So far it has been over 2,729 years since the Israelites were taken out of the land by the Assyrians. The Jews were driven out of the land in AD 70, and many of them, since 1948, have returned to the land that is called the nation of Israel today. They still are not seeking their God as of today but will be during the tribulation period, shortly after Russia and its allies invade Israel from the north (Ezek. 39:22–25). In verse 25, it mentions "Jacob," and following that, it mentions the "whole house" of Israel. Jacob, Samaria, and Israel are words used in the Scriptures most of the time to refer to the northern kingdom, especially after the kingdoms were divided in 1010 BC. On the other hand, Jerusalem, Judah, and Jews are words that usually described the southern kingdom.

So here is what we should have learned so far: *End-time Babylon* has living within its borders a lot of Jews, and a lot of, I'll call them, "gentiles from the seed of Israel." We may not know them, but our Lord knows every one of them. These two groups of people, not only living in Babylon but all nations containing either or both groups, will be returning to Israel to seek their God from the middle of the tribulation to the end of it, thus escaping being destroyed with Babylon by the judgment of God. A multitude of both seeds will return to the land of Israel to live and worship the Lord. They will eventually fill the land to the original borders that God gave to Abraham. We have covered almost four pages to prove that the text in Jeremiah 50:4 is taking place during the tribulation period so that we could see that the Babylon of Jeremiah 50, and verse 4 is talking about end-time Babylon. **"In those days, and at that time, saith the Lord, the children of Israel shall come, they and the children of Judah together . . ."** I covered this verse earlier in the study, but I wanted you to see that this is taking place during the time that our Lord is judging end-time Babylon. All of Jeremiah 50 and 51 are about this end-time nation that will be leveled by the judgment of almighty God.

In Jeremiah 50:1–4, we can see without a doubt that the Babylon mentioned in this text is end-time Babylon, because verse 4 says the two nations are coming back together to seek the Lord in Israel. Therefore, all that is written in Jeremiah 50 and 51 contain prophecy about the nation called Babylon that will be in existence during the end times. In Isaiah 13 and 14, we see the nation of Babylon mentioned, and once again we need to examine the text to identify whether it's ancient, present-day, or end-time Babylon. The destruction of Babylon in these chapters is easily identified as end-time Babylon, which is being destroyed during the tribulation period, as seen in 13:9–11, which says, **"Behold the day of the Lord cometh . . . For the stars of heaven and the constellations thereof shall not give their light: the sun shall be darkened in his going forth, and the moon shall**

not cause her light to shine. And I will punish the world for their evil . . ."

Compare these Scriptures with those of the New Testament. Revelation 8:12 says, **"And the forth angel sounded, and a third part of the sun was smitten, and the third part of the moon, and the third part of the stars; so as the third part of them was darkened, and the day shone not for a third part of it, and the night likewise."** These verses speak of the end-time judgment that is coming upon the earth during the last three and a half years of the tribulation period. Now that we know the writers in Jeremiah in 50 and 51, Isaiah 13 and 14, and Revelation 18 are all speaking of commercial Babylon of the end time, let's take a look at her characteristics seen in these books and chapters, as they will help us in identifying who she is.

Let's first consider some verses from Jeremiah 50 and 51.

In Jeremiah 50:2, Babylon is mentioned as having a couple of gods over her with the names of Bel and Merodach. Bel is known as the "god of countries." Thus, whoever the end-time nation of Babylon is, she has a natural tendency to rule over other countries.

In Jeremiah 50:12, Babylon has a mother nation that gave birth to her. That is, the people of the mother nation sent their people to live in the location of end-time Babylon, and were responsible for establishing it as a nation. The early settlers came over from the nation of England to America, and the early settlements were and still are called today "New England" in the United States. Thus England, the mother, gave birth to a daughter nation. Am I saying that the United States is end-time Babylon? I would rather not make a statement of that nature at this time in this Bible study, but allow the Scriptures to reveal to you, the reader, who Babylon is.

In Jeremiah 50:12, Babylon is the hindermost of the nations, which means either the least or the last. I doubt that it means the least of the nations when we see in Scripture that she is the glory of the nations (Isa. 13:19). Therefore, it means the last of the nations to come into existence or the newest nation when compared to all the other nations.

In Jeremiah 50:23, Babylon is **"the hammer of the whole earth . . ."** That is, she is the great carpenter that builds the nations of the earth by her influence and might into a world system that's to her liking.

Jeremiah 50:31 says, **"Behold, I am against thee, O thou most proud . . ."** Babylon is a proud nation. Need I say more about this characteristic? She is as proud as proud can be. It is a nation that has everything a person could want, basing this statement upon the eighteenth chapter of the book of Revelation.

Jeremiah 50:32 refers to Babylon with the pronouns in a masculine gender, **"And the most proud shall stumble and fall and none shall raise *him* up: and I will kindle a fire in *his* cities . . ."** Notice that the gender of the pronouns his/him in this verse are masculine, and not as we have seen in most of the past verses we've looked at. In fact, if we look back at verse 15, Babylon is referred to as she. Verse 17 uses the masculine twice: first referring to the past when the northern tribes were attacked and scattered by the king of Assyria—**"The king of Assyria hath devoured him . . ."**—with the word *him* in this verse being Israel, and notice what follows: **"And last *this Nebuchadnezzar* king of Babylon hath broken his bones."** Since we have the word king used here, we know that this noun's gender is masculine. Also notice that *this* Nebuchadnezzar is not the king that existed in 722 BC but the Nebuchadnezzar that will rule the end time Babylon of this text. Jeremiah was not given the name of this end-time king, so he refers to him as this Nebuchadnezzar. Going back to the words in this verse that say, **"And I will kindle a fire in his *cities,"*** we notice that this king of Babylon lives in a nation that has a plurality of cities.

Jeremiah 50:37 says the Lord will bring a sword **"upon all the mingled people that are in the midst of her . . ."** The word *mingled* means mixed, and now we know that Babylon is a nation that has people from many nations living in her cities.

Jeremiah 50:38 says that Babylon is, **"The land of graven images, and they are mad upon their idols,"** and the word mad here also means *insane with*. Thus we can conclude that end-time Babylon is a nation that loves graven images and will not let go of her idols, which her people love and which cause them to continue to be blind to the word of the Lord. They love the things of this world so much that they idolize them. They are worshipers of the creation and the things that men have made rather than the creator who created all things, and if a person puts anything before God, than he/she is a worshipper of an idol.

In Jeremiah 50:42, Babylon is referred to as **"the daughter of Babylon,"** and I do not believe that this refers to the physical seed of Babylon but the "characteristic seed," that is, who, as this great end time nation, has the likeness or characteristics of ancient Babylon? More than likely this Babylon refers to Babel as well as ancient Babylon. Babel can rightfully be called the first Babylon and was Satan's masterpiece, in that he had the world united in total rebellion against God. Everyone was building a tower in one central geographical location instead of obeying God and filling the whole world with people, as God had commanded them to.

The second Babylon in the Scriptures is the ancient city in Iraq with all of its glory, wealth, might, and power. Satan has been moving the people of the world, with its past world empires, toward the day of the birth of the daughter of Babylon past. She will have all the characteristics of the first and second Babylon rolled up into one. She will unite the people of the world together into a one-world government system, and just like ancient Babylon was ruled by the first Nebuchadnezzar, this person in Jeremiah 50:15 is referred to as ". . . *this Nebuchadnezzar . . ."* and will rule from end-time Babylon. Satan will attempt to have everyone in the world worshiping him, in the person of the Antichrist, as God. The nation that he will rule from will have all the characteristics of the original and second Babylon.

Look at Revelation 17:11, **"And the beast that was, and is not, even he is the eight, and is of the seven . . ."** The beast in this verse *that was* refers to the world government system of the first Babylon (Babel). Notice that the eighth head comes from or evolves from the seven before it, or more directly from the seventh head itself, and it is the part of the beast that *shall be*, or the return or rebirth of the beast that existed before the seven heads were in existence. In verse 12, we see the ten horns of the beast giving their power to the person of Antichrist, and again they will do this **"until the words of God shall be fulfilled"** (Rev. 17:17b). In verse 10 of Revelation 18, she is said to be a mighty city, and in verse 7, **"How much she hath glorified herself, and lived deliciously . . ."** Her wealth is seen in verses 12 and 13, and she can purchase anything she wants or craves. The city of Babylon in Iraq was a wealthy city with great beauty, and a great defense with walls around it that chariots could ride on the top. Which nation has all of the characteristics of all the past Babylons?

Turn to Jeremiah 51:6, 45. Whoever end-time Babylon is, she contains a lot of *tribulation saints* (people who have believed during the Tribulation Period), and God instructs them to get out of her before he brings judgment upon her. Verse 45 says, **"My people, go ye out of the midst of her, and deliver every man his soul from the fierce anger of the Lord."** I believe that whoever this nation is, she has to be a nation that has heard a lot about the last days or the end-time prophecies of the Bible before she entered the tribulation period. Again Revelation 18:4 says, **"And I heard another voice from heaven, saying, come out of her my people, that ye be not partakers of her sins . . ."**

Jeremiah 51:7 says, **"Babylon hath been a golden cup in the Lord's hand . . ."** Whoever this nation is at the time of her destruction, she was at one time a golden cup in the Lord's hand. Evidently she had been used of the Lord for good on this planet before she became evil or corrupt.

Jeremiah 51:11 says, **"The Lord hath raised up the spirit of the Medes: for his device is against Babylon, to destroy it . . ."** The Lord will use Iran, the Medes of the past, with other nations, to come against end-time Babylon and destroy it to the point where she will never be inhabited again.

[6]From The History of the Medes, "The Medes were an people of <u>Indo-Iranian</u>(Aryan) origin who inhabited the western and north-western portion of *present-day Iran*."

Again verse 28 says, **"Prepare against her the nations with the kings of the Medes . . ."** Now let's do a little thinking together and remember how the Medes and the Persians battled against the Babylon of their day. They couldn't penetrate the mighty walls of the city with any of their weapons, but this didn't defeat them, and they came up with a plan to take Babylon from the inside through damming up the river that ran under the walls and through the city, and they went in under the walls. What a spirit and determination they had to go boldly in and destroy Babylon, the great giant of their day and time. Just like old times, I believe that this will be reenacted with modern-day Iran, and the nations coming with her, against the Babylon of our day.

I believe that the Iranians with the nations coming from the north will come with arrows that won't miss their targets, because their arrows, which refer to the weapons of modern-day warfare, will be planted inside end-time Babylon to explode simultaneously just before the enemy enters in to complete the job God has sent them to do. The city of Babylon past had great protection around it, and the enemy had to penetrate the city from the dried-up river bed, which allowed them to enter the city and take it from the inside. Today, America has the greatest defenses with our military, satellites, and weapons of war that the only way someone could possibility defeat us would be the crippling of our military bases from the inside first. The nation that defeated the city of Babylon (the Medes) is the one that will defeat us (Iran is the Medes). Déjà vu!

Jeremiah 50:9 says, **"For, lo, I will raise and cause to come up against Babylon an assembly of great nations from the north country . . . their arrows shall be as of a mighty expert man; none shall return in vain."** A person might say, but how do I know this isn't ancient Babylon spoken of in this text? Just examine the surrounding verses; first, there were only two nations that captured ancient Babylon, and they were the Medes and the Persians, but there are many nations mentioned in this text, and second, verse 12 says this Babylon had a mother nation that gave birth to her. Ancient Babylon grew into existence through the people who remained in the area after God scattered the rest into other parts of the world at the Tower of Babel. Also, this Babylon will be completely destroyed and never be inhabited again (Jer. 51:64). Ancient Babylon was defeated but not destroyed, and it exists today in Iraq as a city.

Jeremiah 51:13 says, **"Oh thou that dwelleth upon many waters, abundant in treasures . . ."** Whoever end-time Babylon is, she has her people in many nations, most likely in military bases around the world. The word "waters" is symbolic for nations or peoples in prophecy. Neither ancient Babylon nor the Tower of Babel were ever located in different countries like this Babylon is. The United States has over one hundred bases (army, USAF, marine, or naval) in forty-seven different nations or islands around the world. We have our military personal stationed in these forty-seven different nations or islands.

Let's look at Jeremiah 51:24, 35, 49. Verse 24 says, **"All the evil that they have done in Zion . . ."** Babylon will allow and be the cause of evil to come upon the inhabitants of Jerusalem. Verse 35 says, **"The violence done to me** [Israel] **and my flesh be upon Babylon . . ."** Verse 49 says, **"As Babylon hath caused the slain of Israel to fall, so at Babylon shall fall the slain of all the earth."** She also will be the cause of many in Israel to be slain by the weapons of war. So this end-time giant, who was once a golden cup in the Lord's hand, will turn against God's people in Zion and side with her enemies. The United States has been Israel's best ally, but we can see at this very moment in time that we are slowly turning our back on Israel and siding with the Palestinians to divide the land into two nations, which is against the word of God.

Jeremiah 51:30 says, **"The mighty men of Babylon have forborne to fight . . ."** or ceased fighting. From Webster's online dictionary, "to hold oneself back from, especially withhold effort"[7] Even though this end-time nation has a mighty military, they are weakened by a sudden attack that she, with her pride, was not expecting, and her men of war become frightened and weakened as women. Jeremiah 50:31 says, **"Behold, I am against thee, O thou most proud . . ."** She is a nation with great pride, as seen throughout the books, and chapters we are using for this Bible study.

Jeremiah 51:53 says, **"Though Babylon should mount up to heaven** [into space], **and though she should fortify the height of her strength . . ."** Whoever this end-time nation is, she has increased the strength of her might, and her military forces are the strongest by use of the heavens, atmospheric and stellar. This would indicate that she has heavenly weapons, like ICBMs, sophisticated airplanes, and satellites that make her more powerful offensively and defensively than the other nation. Jeremiah 50:24 says, **"I have laid a snare for thee, and thou art also taken, O Babylon, and thou wast not aware . . ."** Jeremiah 50:30b says, **"Their might hath failed; they became as women . . ."** She will be weakened through an attack that she was not aware of, and this will cripple her and cause her army to be weakened to the point that they are said to be like women.

Jeremiah 51:41 says, **"How is Sheshach** [a word that refers to Babylon] **taken! and how is the praise of the whole earth surprised! how is Babylon become an astonishment among the nations!"** This verse isn't really asking a question but making the statement that this great end-time nation, which all the other nations look up to, because she is the praise of the whole earth, has been surprised, and the nations are astonished at her demise. The nations of this world would have never thought that this great end-time nation would ever be destroyed! They are astonished that this great nation, with all its wealth and military power, being the voice and hammer of the earth, full of pride, standing tall, full of all the idols that others crave, has been destroyed.

Jeremiah 51:55 is a reference to Babylon being the great voice. **"Because the Lord hath spoiled** [plundered] **Babylon, and destroyed out of her the great voice . . ."** This nation will have, and does have today, a great voice in this present world. When she speaks, the others listen and respond, either with her or against her, but she has the greatest voice on this current planet.

Jeremiah 51:64 says, **"Thus shall Babylon sink, and shall not rise from the evil that I will bring upon her . . ."** This is a verse of Scripture that refers to end-time Babylon and not ancient Babylon, for the Lord says that he will destroy Babylon to the point that it will never rise again. Ancient Babylon, which was defeated by the Medes and Persians, was taken over from the invading army from the inside but never destroyed and was still in existence when Peter took the gospel to it in the first century

The Destruction of America Is Coming Soon

(1 Pet. 5:13). In Peter's salutation at the end of 1 Peter, he says in verse 13, **"The church that is at Babylon, elected together with you, saluteth you; and so does Marcus my son."** This was over two hundred years later when he wrote about the church in Babylon. Here is an example of how one verse in Scripture helps us identify a true interpretation of a text. Comparing Scripture with Scripture, here a little there a little, line upon line, etc.

Now let's go to Isaiah 13 and 14 to see what they say about end-time Babylon.

Isaiah 13:1–2 says, **"The burden of Babylon, which Isaiah the son of Amoz did see. Lift up a banner upon the high mountain..."** We see here that Babylon is called a high mountain. Whenever we see a mountain mentioned in Scripture, we need to study the text to find out whether it's a literal mountain, or a figurative one, because when the text demands a symbolic interpretation, than the mountain has to be figurative. Likewise, when the text demands a literal interpretation, we must see the mountain as a literal one. Other places in Scripture where mountains are nations instead of literal mountains are: Isaiah 25:6, 7, 10; 2:2; 11:9; and Revelation 17:9. Isaiah 25:6 says, **"And in this mountain shall the Lord of hosts make unto all people a feast of fat things . . ."** It is speaking of Israel as a mountain that the Lord will be in when he brings in the feast of the millennium. Notice he is not *on* a mountain, but *in* it. Also, in verses seven and ten, he (God) is *in* the mountain (nation of Israel) of the coming kingdom.

Isaiah 2:2 says, **"And it shall come to pass in the last days, that the mountain** [nation or kingdom] **of the Lord's house shall be established in the top of the mountains, and shall be exalted above the hills; and all nations shall flow unto it."** Here we see the use of the words *mountain* and *mountains* used symbolically. The word *mountain* means the kingdom that will rule all the nations. When it says in the top of the mountains, it means he rules over all nations from Israel where his kingdom has been established as promised to David. Isaiah 11:9 says, **"They shall not hurt nor destroy *in* all my holy mountain: for the earth shall be full of the knowledge of the Lord . . ."**

Again, this is a reference to the coming kingdom of God in Israel, and it is called a mountain.

Now, follow me to Revelation 17:9, **"And here is a mind which hath wisdom. The seven heads are seven mountains [nations] on which the woman sitteth."** Contrary to the modern-day teaching that these mountains are the seven hills in Rome, they are the six past nations that ruled the world, with one to come. If we fail to interpret this verse correctly, then the vast majority of our interpretation of end-time prophecy with its key players will be in error. Go back to chapter 1 if you need to refresh your mind about the seven mountains. The seventh mountain (kingdom) is modern-day Babylon, and she brings into existence a world government system called in the Bible "the beast with ten horns," Below, we are going to see that the Antichrist rules from her!

Back to Isaiah 13:14. Let's take a look into these verses, as they will reveal what nation the Antichrist will rule the world from. In Isaiah 14:3-7, right after the Lord gives Israel rest at the end of the tribulation period, he tells them in verse 4 to, **"Take up a proverb against the king of Babylon . . ."** and in verse six he says, **"He who smote the people in wrath with a continual stroke, he that ruled the nations in anger, is persecuted, and none hindereth."** Beloved in Christ, the Antichrist will rule the world from end-time Babylon. We see both the fall of Satan and the Antichrist in verses 12 through 17, with Satan being mentioned in the first four verses and the Antichrist in the next two. Remember that Satan will indwell the Antichrist from the middle of the Daniel's seventieth week to its end.

So now we can see clearly that the key player and nation in end-time prophecy is the Antichrist ruling from end-time Babylon. Even though he is of the seed of the Roman Empire, he will not rule from Rome or Europe. May our Lord give to you wisdom, knowledge, and understanding as we move along in Scripture to see that the Antichrist will *not* rule from a nation in Europe from the "revived Roman empire," including ten of its nations or kings. To see this truth, we must go to the book of the Revelation of Jesus Christ and look deeply into the most important verses and interpret them correctly, in order to see the balance of the key players of end-time prophecy.

We'll do so after looking at some more characteristics of end-time Babylon in Isaiah 13 and 14.

Isaiah 13:1 says she is a **"high mountain,"** figuratively meaning a great and mighty nation lifted high above others.

Isaiah 13:4 says there will be a **"multitude of mountains,"** meaning many people from many nations. Later in the verse, these nations will be gathered together to battle against Babylon. Remember, we already covered from the Scriptures that the people of Iran, along with several other Arab nations, will destroy end-time Babylon.

In Isaiah 13:5, the people who come to destroy her will come from a far country or a distant land to do battle with end-time Babylon, and this verse says they will destroy the whole land. This verse will help us in the elimination of ancient Babylon being this mighty end-time nation, as verse 17 mentions the *Medes* being involved as the leading nation that comes against Babylon. The *Medes* are the *Iranians* of today, and the nation of Iran is right next to Iraq, where today's ancient Babylon exists. Now look again at 5 five where it says, **"They come from a *far country*, from the end of heaven, even the Lord, and the weapons of his indignation, to destroy** [end- time Babylon] **the whole land."** Now let's reason together. If ancient Babylon is the great Babylon of the end times, this verse would be a lie! Why? because ancient Babylon is located in Iraq and is the neighboring nation of Iran. Thus the Medes would not be coming from a far country.

Isaiah 13:19 says Babylon is **"the glory of the kingdoms, the beauty of the Chaldees' excellency . . ."** This is similar to how Jesus Christ is our glory, and we look to him for our answers to life and live under his power to be like him. End-time Babylon will be the glory of all the kingdoms, and the others will look to her for their answers. She is also the beauty of the people who inhabit her and have made her great in their own eyes. So self-centered is she that she cannot see her great sins that have mounted up to heaven. She is so full of pride and so blind that she cannot see the coming judgment of God. Other kingdoms admire her beauty and glory and desire to be like her.

Isaiah 14:4-6 says, **"That thou shalt take up this proverb against the king of Babylon, and say, How hath the oppressor ceased!"** The golden city ceased! Again there are no questions being asked here but strong statements about the end of both the Antichrist's rule, and his golden city, which are no more. The word *city* is used 866 times in the Bible, but only once is it translated this way in this verse. In the Hebrew the word used is *madhebah*, taken from *Strong's Exhaustive Concordance of the Bible*[3], and it means "gold making," meaning something greater than the refining of gold, and it's centered on the wealth of this rich, money-making nation. There is no other city or civil empire like it in the world.

When we get to the book of the Revelation, we'll see the wealth of this mighty nation. In verse 5, the Lord has broken the staff of the wicked and destroyed the scepter of the rulers. Verse 6 says **"He** [the Antichrist] **smote the people in wrath with a continual stroke, he that ruled the nations in anger, is persecuted, and none hindereth."** When we read these verses and study them in the remainder of this chapter, keeping everything in context, we'll see that the Antichrist is ruling from that great end-time nation called Babylon. Just these verses alone prove that the king of Babylon will be the Antichrist, the oppressor of the nations that ruled in anger. Remember that he is not doing this by himself but with the power of Satan who indwells him and with ten other kings under his authority **"until the word's of God be fulfilled"** (Rev. 17:17).

Isaiah 14:7–11 says that after Babylon is destroyed, **"The whole earth is at rest..."** We need only to look at the preceding verses to see why the whole earth is at rest.

Isaiah 14:12–23 describes the fall of the Antichrist, indwelt by Satan at the end of the tribulation period, along with Babylon's destruction. Actually, it is not just a fall but a casting down of Satan to the pit as seen in verse 15. The fall is a reference to Satan, who wants to be like "the most high" (God), as seen in verse 13. In Revelation 12:9–10, we see Satan being cast out of heaven and down to the earth to indwell the Antichrist for the last three and a half years and for the purpose of being worshipped by the world. **"And the great dragon was cast out, that old serpent, called the Devil, and Satan . . . for the accuser of our brethren is cast down . . ."** This is done in the middle of the Daniel's last week, and Satan has just three and one half years left to gather people to worship him, and he goes on a rampage during those last 1,260 days, which are also known as the great tribulation period or the time of Jacob's trouble, during which we see the seventh seal, the trumpet, and vial judgments take place. A Jewish calendar year equals 360 days, and thus 1,260 days equal three and a half years.

Let's move on to the book of Revelation, where we'll see a lot more of the characteristics of end-time Babylon that will help us identify her. We are going to study chapter 18, where we see the nation's civil authority, not the religious authority, which we have already seen in chapter 17.

Revelation 18:3 says, **"For all the nations have drunk the wine of her wrath of her fornication, and the kings of the earth have committed fornication with her, and the merchants of the earth are waxed** [became] **rich through the abundance of her delicacies."** Now this is going to take a little thinking on our part. First, let's not take anything out of context. First the word fornication does not mean sexual fornication but spiritual fornication. This fornication is against the God who created us. That is, this great end-time nation has caused many nations to depend upon its buying power and has created an idolatrous system with other nations, in which all are guilty of the worship of things instead of God.

You know and I know that things that are great to look at and things we crave are nice to have, but all of these feed the lust of the flesh, the lust of the eyes, and the pride of life, which are the very heart or desires of our sinful nature. It's the unsaved people I'm pointing at here, but it is possible for a Christian to love the world more than he/she loves God. First John 2:15–16 says, **"Love not the world, neither the things that are in the world. If any man love the world, the love of the Father is not in him. For all that is in the world, the lust of the flesh, and the lust of the eyes, and the pride of life, is not of the Father,** but is of the world." In 2 Timothy 4:10, the apostle Paul said, **"For Demus hath forsaken me, having loved this present world, and is departed unto Thessalonica . . ."**

Revelation 18:4 says, **"Come out of her, my people, that ye be not partakers of her sins, and that ye receive not her plagues."** Babylon has a lot of tribulation saints within her borders, and God is warning them to depart. I believe that the United States will be a nation that will have many tribulation period saints in her during the end-time judgment of the nations, due to the current sharing of the Scriptures by believers with unbelievers during our day. In other words, because the Word of God is shared in abundance today, there will be a big harvest ready after the rapture of the Church, and many will come to Christ for salvation.

Revelation 18:5 says the sins of Babylon have reached into heaven: **"For her sins have reached unto heaven, and God hath remembered her iniquities."** This great nation called Babylon will be full of sins against the God of heaven. This verse speaks about the abundance of her sins and the fact that they have mounted up to heaven. Take a look at some of the sins of America: the killing of babies (50,000 a year) in the womb, gambling in many states, homosexuality, same-sex marriage, idolatry, the love of money, pornography, and idolatry, we allow the worship of any god, many men and women are living together in sin, children born out of wedlock, and on and on goes the list. I believe that in God's eyes, America is the most sinful nation in the world, and that is why we are going to be judged. We say that we are a Christian nation, but our actions show that we aren't.

Revelation 18:7 says, **"How much she hath glorified herself, and lived deliciously, [luxuriously] so much torment and sorrow give her: for she saith in her heart, I sit as a queen, and am no widow, and shall see no sorrow."** This great end-time nation is very rich, and the people in her live more richly above the other people in this world, which causes her to be full of pride and glorify herself. She also has a false sense of security that makes her believe she is safe and secure from the harm that others could bring upon her. She believes that she sits as the queen over the world.

Revelation 18:8 says that because of the above, she will come to her end by the judgment of almighty God in one day. **"Therefore shall her plagues come in one day . . . she shall be utterly burned with fire . . ."** Compare with Isaiah 13:19–22, where verse 19 starts with, **"Babylon, the glory of the kingdoms . . . shall be as when God overthrew Sodom and Gomorrah."** And how did God over throw them? Answer, by fire in one day. Verse 20 says, **"It shall never be inhabited . . ."** along with the rest of verses 21 and 22. Compare with Jeremiah 51:8, **"Babylon is suddenly fallen and destroyed . . ."** And once more compare with Revelation 18:17, **"For in one hour so great riches is come to naught . . ."** and again Revelation 18:10, **"For in one hour is thy judgment come."**

Revelation 18:11–19 shows us the great wealth of this end-time nation and gives us an idea of her location or where she is. She has seaports where many ships bring their goods to sell to her people, and verse 15 says the buying of these goods makes the merchants of other nations rich. In this verse, the merchants are also seen crying aboard their ships when they see mighty Babylon burning with fire from afar off. And once again, this verse quickly rules out any thought that Iraq's Babylon could possibly be this end-time nation. The nearest body of water to the city of Babylon in Iraq is 350 miles away, and thus she has no seaports. Look at the things that this end-time nation can afford to buy in verses 12 through 14. Did you know that the United States imports over 70 percent of the world's goods?

Revelation 18:21 says that when Babylon is destroyed, she will never be inhabited with human beings again: **"Thus with violence shall that great city Babylon be thrown down, and shall be found no more at all."** Do not be confused by the word *city* as we think of a city today. This is not just the end of one city in one nation, and the word *city* here represents a civil authority, the people of the whole land where the nation exists. When we look in the Old Testament, we see that Babylon contains many cities within her borders. In Jeremiah 51:31, we see the description of what is taking place within the borders of Babylon as she is being judged by God. It says, **"One post shall** run to meet another and one messenger to meet another, to show the king of Babylon that *his city* is taken at one end."

Jeremiah 51:42–42 continues, **"The sea is come up upon Babylon: she is covered with the multitude of the waves thereof. Her cities are desolation, a dry land, and a wilderness, a land wherein no man dwelleth, neither doth any son of man pass thereby."** The sea mentioned with its waves in verse 42 does not mean literal water but is symbolic for people and is to be taken figuratively, just like in Revelation 13:1 where the beast comes up out of the sea. Here it means the sea of people that will come as a wave and cover Babylon after the fiery judgment of what will most likely be the timely setting off of suitcase nukes near all her important cities and military bases. Note in the next verse of Jeremiah 43 where it says, **"Her cities are a desolation, a *dry* land . . ."** If we take verse 42 to be a literal interpretation of water, then what verse 43 says can't be true.

Revelation 18:22 says there will be no more music (goodbye "American Idol") coming out of Babylon and no more crafts or businesses operating. In next verse, there are no more candles being lit, and marriages have ceased. God is letting us know that Babylon is without electricity, and there isn't even a candle being lit, as there are no people to light one.

Revelation 18:23 says, **"For by her sorceries were all the nations deceived."** When looking up the meaning of the word sorcery, we find it to mean magical power and charm, and when we use these definitions of the word in this context, it means that Babylon was able to deceive all the nations through her magical charm. That is, she charmed and persuaded them into going her way, and she had the magical power and influence to do so. Remember that she is both the voice and the hammer of the whole earth.

Revelation 18:24 says, **"And in her was found the blood of the prophets, and of the saints, and all that were slain upon the earth."** You might be thinking that there were no prophets slain in the United States, but God looks at Babylon past, present, and future when he makes this statement. We are Babylon future, and we will be responsible for slaying many saints during the tribulation period. Many of them will be in prisons, and the Antichrist will not release them. In Isaiah 14:16, the Antichrist is looked upon as the man who made the earth to tremble. This precedes the statement in the next verse where it ends saying, **"That opened not the house of his prisoners."** Is the reader aware that there are over six hundred prisons in America's military bases with barbed wire around them that are totally empty of people and all built in recent years? These prisons are there to lock up the rebellious people who won't accept the one world government or the Antichrist as god. Do a web search on prison confines at military bases in America to view this fact.

To close this chapter with the question, *who is end-time Babylon?* there is no other nation in the world today other than the great nation of the United States of America that matches every characteristic of end-time Babylon from the Scripture. There is no doubt about my spiritual conviction that it is the nation of America, in which I was blessed to be born and where I live, that will become, after the church is taken out by our Lord, that great and mighty nation known as end-time Babylon.

When I think of the blindness of this nation, and especially the church (born-again believers) today, there is a lack of study in God's word. I know that the devil and his demons deceived me in 1988. They have done a great job in deceiving the world and the church concerning what is about to happen very soon. The church is looking for a person to rise up in Europe as the Antichrist, and they are scratching their heads concerning the role of the United States in the end-time prophecy. All they have to do is get into their Bibles that they carry to worship services every Sunday and study the word of God. The Bible says in 2 Timothy 2:15, **"Study to show thyself approved unto God, a *workman* that needeth not to be ashamed, *rightly* dividing the word of truth."** See the word workman in the verse above? Well, that is the problem in today's sleeping church. In other words, they are not working at studying their Bibles, and that is the reason why Satan has them deceived. Lord, Lord, I pray, open our eyes that we may see your truth rightly divided.

If you want to be prepared for what is coming upon the earth, you'll need a right standing with Jesus Christ by being born again. If you have never been spiritually reborn, go to a fundamental Christian church where someone can lead you into this blessed experience. Then you can look this coming global disaster straight in the eye with the complete assurance that you will not be here to see the judgment of God, as the Bible gives assurance that born-again believers will be spared the agony of having to go through this terrible period.

If you are already a believer, you need to redouble your efforts to witness to others around you about Jesus Christ and the salvation God offers and pray for the unsaved to come to the place where they are believers. My prayer is that anyone who reads this book, and the enclosed written words of God, may have his or her spiritual eyes opened from a deep sleep to see where we are at this very moment of history or *His Story*.

If you are reading this book and do not know Jesus Christ as your personal savoir, the Bible says that we are all under sin. That is, everyone is born with a sin nature, and that sin nature separates us from our holy God. But he made a sacrifice for us that satisfy his holiness, and that sacrifice was made at the cross when his son Jesus Christ died to take away our sins. When we believe what Jesus did for each one of us *(you and me)*—yes, you are included—the moment we believe what God did for us, we become his children (born-again), and we can communicate with him through prayer. Read John 3:16. He loves you and wants you to come to him. Turn away from yourself by giving him control of your life and your sinning ways and turn to him.

Once you are saved, you might want to read the gospel of John and start going to a good, Bible-teaching church.

Endnotes

[1] All Bible quotes, *The King James Study Bible*, Thomas Nelson 1798

[2] *Gale Encyclopedia of World Governments*, http://www.gale.cengage.com/pdf/facts/GaleEnclcWorldHistory-pdf

[3] *Strong's Exhaustive Concordance of the Bible*, James Strong, Thomas Nelson, Nashville, TN

[4] *Illustrated History of the Roman Empire* (internet search) http://www.roman-empire.net

[5] *Arbatel of Magic*, translated into English by Robert Turner, London 1655

[6] *History of the Medes*, www.taroscopes.com

[7] Webster's online dictionary, Merriam-webster.com